Lily Pads

Stories of God on Display

Judith,
You are His Masterpiece (Eph 2:10)
loved lavishly I John 3:1

*Hearing the Voice of God in
Everyday Situations and in
Everyday Life*

D1166293

Copyright

Scriptures taken from the Holy Bible, New International Version®, NIV®. Copyright © 1973, 1978, 1984, 2011 by Biblica, Inc.™ Used by permission of Zondervan. All rights reserved worldwide. www.zondervan.com The "NIV" and "New International Version" are trademarks registered in the United States Patent and Trademark Office by Biblica, Inc.™

The ESV Global Study Bible®, ESV® Bible
Copyright © 2012 by Crossway.
All rights reserved.

The Holy Bible, English Standard Version® (ESV®)
Copyright © 2001 by Crossway,
a publishing ministry of Good News Publishers.
All rights reserved.
ESV Text Edition: 2011

© Rachel Inouye, 2016

All rights reserved. No part of this book is to be copied or used for any use without the expressed written consent of the author. 2016.

Dedication

This book is dedicated to...

The Lord Jesus who loves me with an everlasting and lavish love and purchased me with His blood. My identity is in You. I'm so grateful that You drew me to yourself early and I hear Your tender voice of love. You speak to me even through a lily pad. I'm so thankful!

Michael, you are a loving husband and my best friend. I'm so glad I said yes to your marriage proposal. You make me radiant. Your hard work allows me the time to speak, minister, mentor and write. I respect you highly and love you deeply.

Michael, Andrew and Grace when I began this book you encouraged me, "Mom, go for it!" I appreciate you more than you will ever know. You're each a gift from the LORD and a sign of His abundant favor toward me. I'm proud of you and 1 absolutely love being your mom. Amy, I'm so thankful you're an Inouye.

Mom and Dad, you are simply OUTSTANDING constant cheerleaders and prayer warriors in my life! I love and respect you both so much. Your influence in my life and impact on my walk of faith can't be measured this side of heaven, but one day we will see it clearly. I love being your baby girl.

Barb, Sharon and Joyce, I don't take family unity for granted, as you know, and I'm beyond thrilled that I have the close relationship that I do with each of you. Your support of all I do and who I am is unwavering. You are beautiful treasures and you are my life heroes.

My friends, God has used you to shape and form me through your love, acceptance, support, prayers and encouragement. Thanks for spurring me on to love and good deeds. Let's have coffee!

Victoria, you are simply the BEST! I don't know if this book would ever had been birthed without you as its editing midwife.

Pam, thank you for scrubbing the text one last time and encouraging me after reading it by saying when you read it, it was as if we were having coffee together.

Lily Pad: The cover of this book I painted years ago while attending a summer acrylic painting class that my father Richard Heggen taught in my home state of Iowa. I first photographed the water lilies in Park Rapids, Minnesota. The painting now hangs in my daughter Grace's bedroom.

Contents

Foreword

I'm so delighted for you, dear reader! What you hold in your hands is a gift of encouragement from a woman supremely gifted in encouraging. I first met Rachel 30 years ago in a young marrieds group at our church in Chicagoland. She was the one who winsomely stood out on a summer Sunday morning in a bright (and I mean bright!) fuchsia dress. Through the years, I have loved being able to laugh and pray together, to beat our husbands in a game of Rook at least once, to bear witness to her faithful parenting of her three remarkable children (and now one lovely in-law), to watch her spiritual influence flourish. Rachel continues to stand out in my life as an exceptional woman wholly devoted to vibrant worship and pointing others to the Lord Jesus...ever-so-brightly, winsomely, humbly. I respect her deeply and cherish the innumerable times in our friendship that God has used her Scripture-laced words to lovingly draw me closer to His heart. I pray for you that, by His Spirit, He would do the same for your heart.

Elizabeth Cole

Director of Connecting
Oakwood Church

Introduction

It's not that complicated: God didn't just write a book and then stop speaking. He still speaks! This book includes some of the finite ways that the infinite God communicates. Lily Pads is a collection of regular life short stories laced with scripture. These tangible truths from my daily life have helped me understand God better. Lily pads contains visual ways the invisible God reminds me of His presence. It's the practice of listening to the voice of God. It's the treasure hunt of looking for God in everything.

The stories are random yet connected because they are about times God has taught me truth, spoken or revealed Himself to me. He uses the physical things to teach me about the spiritual and the natural to show me the supernatural. God is on display all around me. He speaks to me. One day He used a lily pad.

I've wondered, as I've written this book, if the illustrations and stories are too simple. When I bounced the idea of this book off people, many gave me encouragement, even confirmation that they'd relate to simple uncomplicated stories. "Sounds like something I'd read!" they said. Well, I sure hope so!

I know that God, in Jesus Christ, came to earth to show us the way to the Father. He spoke and taught using the simple things all around. I see places all over the new testament where Jesus used the common things to explain deep spiritual truths. He talked about soil, a lost coin, one lost sheep, grains of wheat, sheep and goats, yeast and dough, gates and even a mustard seed.

My hope is to share encouragement and truth without making it complicated. I just want to share the good news about the things that God is doing in my life in natural ways. Truth is incredibly profound, but it doesn't have to be complicated. God uses the tangible physical things in this world to reinforce and teach me the deep spiritual truths that I have found in His word. If I am available and ready to see and listen He speaks. I'm amazed at His teaching method, He goes from my eyes and ears to my heart and spirit.

I desire to encourage people. That's the reasons for this book. I hope that when you read a chapter or even the whole book, you will be encouraged that there is an awesome, almighty God who loves you. Greatest news ever! His love is not earned by anything you do. His love for you is not lost because of anything you've done. God isn't just loving, God is love! God loves you so much he came for you in Jesus Christ to make a way for you to know him too. He came that we may have life, life to the full. It's not complicated He still speaks. I know, He even used a floating lily pad to speak to me.

One

Lily Pads

I learned a short, simple song when I was three or four years old. When company came over, my dad and I would sing it for them together. He'd play the guitar, seated on the couch. I'd stand proudly right beside him, with one short leg swinging like a pendulum to the tune's beat and my tiny hand resting on his arm. We'd both sing but my dad would let me shine. I'd brush my bangs aside, grin and sing in my high-pitched childish voice:

"I'm a little white duck swimmin' in the water. A little white duck, doing what he ought-er. Took a bite of a lily pad, flapped his wings and then he said, 'I'm glad,' that I'm a little white duck, swimmin' in the water, quack, quack, quack!"

The song repeats. Same tune but the following verses switch from the little, white duck, to the little, green frog and little, black fly, etc. I always loved singing with my dad and I loved singing the line, "took a bite of the lily pad."

Why lily pads?

Well, I've always liked them. Their broad green leaves stretching across the surface of the water and their water lilies bursting out from below. Their flowers bloom boldly in the sunshine! They thrive in the murky, green, mossy, algae-infested water. Each prominent white bloom sticks its head above the water as if announcing, "Notice me!" Stunning! Isn't that the way I should bloom and shine in this world?

I promise, the things I write about really happened. The word of God is my bread of life. As I read His word, the Bible, He speaks, then teaches me in visual ways, through my life circumstances and daily situations. God even taught me through the lily pad. You see, I'm like a lily pad, in a sense. Lily pads float on the water, rest on top of the substance that sustains them. Sort of a picture of me resting on God's love, mercy, goodness and faithfulness. The water: His all-sustaining power upholding me to spread out and bloom, boldly.

Lily pads cover the entire water's surface, laying beside the next, like puzzle pieces spread a top a table, waiting for their proper placement. That's the way the stories and chapters in this book will be.

These chapters may be related, touch on similar elements, yet this isn't a memoir. It is a compilation of stories written to illustrate how God visually teaches me through my "spiritual eyes" and speaks to me through my "spiritual ears." His truth then sinks down into my heart. Random? Yes! But one theme runs throughout: the tangible teachings of my God on display.

He taught me visually with the lily pad, but it doesn't have to be a lily pad, whatever I've been reading, it seems, comes alive in "pop up" form. I learn, I grow, as these truths are imprinted on my heart and His word saturates my soul. God is on display and speaking everywhere! *"Here I am! Rachel, notice Me!"* I see Him in the morning sunrise, in the glow from the reddish-orange sunset; the autumn leaves turning color; the lusty cry of a newborn; the softness of a child's dimpled hand; the voice of a tenor soloist; or the whirling wings of the humming bird. Everywhere! *"I am God on display!"*

When I tune in, slow down to listen and watch Him, I notice and hear God in the big and small things of life. He is as close to me as my dad on the couch strumming his guitar as we sing together, "Little White Duck." He desires to sing a duet with me too, the duet of the song of my very life. Scripture says He sings over me!

I realize we all have different brains and different learning styles. When I speak to Bible study groups, women come up and ask for my outline. (I guess they think my brain thinks in outline form.) I tell them I don't have one because I could never stick to one. So, instead, the study administrators provide blank paper when I speak.

"Ladies, don't panic," I've told entire audiences, you don't have an outline because there ISN'T one. You see, there isn't ANY-

THING about my brain that thinks in outline form. Nothing! My brain and its thought patterns are more like having a collection of different colored jump ropes lying on stage in a tangled pile. If the ropes represented my points, when I notice one, let's say a pink rope, I pick it up and talk about that for a while. Then I may keep the pink one or I may look down and notice *"Oh, there's a bright, green jump rope!"* So I pick *it* up. I may or may not warn you that I've made the switch. In my mind the pink and bright green ropes share a knot and the ropes are tied, interconnected. So the illustrations and stories are related in MY mind, but they may not always be connected in yours. Make sense?

Many women have reassured me that they think this way, too. Elizabeth, a dear friend, told me women are able to dialogue in "lily pad" format. We track with one another, jumping from thought to thought, just like a frog sitting on one lily pad leaping to another, and then hopping back again. (I mentioned this dialogue concept, this way of communication, to my sweet friend Melanie one day while sitting in my loft area drinking tea, talking about writing this book, she startled me as she exclaimed, "I know what you should call it! You should title it, Lily Pads!")

Sometimes, okay, maybe often, my thoughts don't get completed. I'm talking to a friend, or an audience of women, telling a story, when all of a sudden, I cannot remember an actor's name in the movie I am trying to describe. So, I pause and just move on, saying, "Man, I can't think of his name! Okay, never mind! I'll probably remember it later" And later, mid-sentence, I'll pause and exclaim, "Tom Cruise! It was Tom Cruise!" My friend or the female audience members' heads nod – *"Oh, I got it! Tom Cruise, the actor you were trying to figure out twenty minutes ago, but couldn't remember at the time."* This communicates, *"Message received"* and I can leap back to try to complete my previous thought. So, like a frog, I invite you to jump from lily pad to lily pad with me.

This book is the pick up and put down kind. No lengthy stream of consciousness required so if you put it down to fix a meal, respond to your chiming phone that notifies you of a new text, or chase your kids around for a while you can come back and pick it up! You won't have to re-read huge sections to get back into it, you can lily pad while reading Lily Pads!

God's word* will be mentioned, alluded to, and quoted in these chapters. Jesus is the reason for my life. Jesus is the one that sustains me and I hope to testify to His goodness and glory throughout this book. I hope you will track with me. I know I'm on the planet to encourage people. I hope you will feel encouraged by reading this book.

Two

Music Spilling Out and Over

I was sitting at the table on the back deck to write this book when I heard music streaming from my son Andrew's bedroom window. Not the common loud booming bass of a teenager driving by in some jacked up car. This was beautiful, complicated and originally composed music that spilled out into the air around me and my home. That day he was editing his original EP that he wrote. I marveled at Andrew's music and his incredible gifts of writing lyrics, composing, and editing audio.

I was physically and emotionally drawn into the house. I must admit, it wasn't just the music that drew me inside. I had three reasons: First, because I've had an iced coffee while I've been writing so I need to go to the bathroom; second, I'm eager to hear more, I'm loving the way this song is coming along and developing, I've heard it from its inception; and third, I desperately want to go into his bedroom solely to encourage him. He is truly gifted. I wondered does he know that?

So, I knocked on his door. I was invited in. I opened the door, found Andrew seated on the floor, crossed legged like a twisted pretzel, with the recording microphone pointed down low. He had a mallet poised ready to strike the bright, primary-colored, instrument held both in his hand and against his feet.

This cylindrical, bamboo instrument was purchased from the streets of Guatemala while shopping in Antigua; it was selected to add additional percussion to the song. Fun stuff! His new, fun song was about a cross-country road trip he took a few summers ago.

I dearly love that kid. My eyes burn with tears and my throat constricts as I think about how much I love him. My heart is filled. My thankful prayer erupts. *Thanks Lord Jesus for the gift of Andrew. Thank you for the gifts You've given him. May he always praise the Giver of the gifts.*

The joy that it brings me to watch Andrew do his thing makes me think of how God has wired each of us to do something unique. Something in His kingdom, for His glory. He has wired each of us specifically. God delights in watching us do our thing. It can be hard to identify "our thing" at times because it seems so natural to us. I love to speak in front of and with people. Whether the masses, or a few sweet women while drinking a cup of coffee or sipping some tea, I delight in the privilege of getting to pray for and with young people or a sweet trusted friend. Maybe that's not your thing, but these are desires God has put in me, called me to do, and He's also equipped me to do them. These things bring me great fulfillment, I feel alive while doing them and God delights in doing them through me too!

How cool is that?

I was overwhelmed with the sense of delight that God has when He sees his kids do what He's called and wired them to do. This hit me in a fresh way months ago: The "physical" impressing on me the "spiritual." The love and delight I felt for Andrew highlighted God's great, abundant love for me. He has that same love for you also.

Lily Pad: One wintery, Sunday morning while I sat in the church pew, I watched a video that Andrew had acted in, composed music for, performed the instrumentation on, and edited all of its footage. I looked up at the big video screen projectors, along with the rest of the congregation and tears began to stream down my cheeks! At first I didn't even know it! Next, I sobbed – quietly. I know I didn't watch with the same eyes as the rest of the congregation. I was a proud mom, delighted to see the culmination of so many things Andrew was designed to do, demonstrated before my eyes and ears.

A woman in the section near me approached me after the service asking, "That was your son Andrew, right? I bet you were touched to see that." I told her, "You have NO idea!" I understand, on some small scale, how delighted God is when He sees us do the things we were designed to do with our great pleasure and for His glory and His kingdom's advancement.

God made Andrew such a handsome kid. He's been given great acting ability, put an interest in film in him, a love for music, composing and editing, and then allowed him to be asked to do ALL of those things in ONE project. It blew me away. Those things that he truly loves coalesced into a three minute video.

Ephesians 2:10 We are his workmanship created in Christ Jesus to do good works which God prepared in advance for us to do.

Lily Pads

Thanks, God for always teaching me Your ways through things that I experience! You are a God on display in my life. Thanks that tangible reminders of Your Word will and ways become known to me. Oh, and by the way, thanks too for Andrew.

Three

Tooth Fairy and Identity

Is it while in first or second grade that a child loses his first tooth? My kids are all grown now, so I'm not sure exactly what age it is. But when Michael lost his first tooth, we placed it in a small, orange Tupperware container and sealed it carefully with the lid. He held this little container, carried it around with him and he even took it outside. I don't know why, but he took it to the sandbox of our neighbor's yard and Andrew, three years younger, went with Michael too. Unfortunately, Michael's tooth got lost! I don't know how the container was opened. I'm not sure what happened exactly but Michael was devastated. He came home and lamented, "Mom, now what about the Tooth Fairy? You told me all about the Tooth Fairy! Now she won't come!" I suggested we write to the Tooth Fairy to explain what happened. I dictated his words exactly and he drew a picture illustrating the event. It said something like: My tooth is gone. My brother Andrew lost my tooth, and I was tempted to hit him, but I gained self-control. So my mom told me that we could write to the Tooth Fairy. That's my story. The End.

As he spoke and I wrote, I pictured him in the sandbox with his hand raised, ready to WHACK Andrew, but not doing it. Precious!

That was heavy on his little heart that day, so we just wrote it down, folded the paper explanation and we stuck it under his pillow later that night. The Tooth Fairy, lo and behold, left the money.

So when his next tooth fell out of his little mouth he was not frightened at all. Rather he was quite excited about it. He put the tooth under his pillow at night so excitedly because he remembered that he got some cash! But we forgot to go and put money under young Michael's pillow. (Okay, Okay, Okay, time out here! Michael's first tooth was LOST, a somewhat traumatic event. You would think I'd be AWARE. I know, I know, but I just spaced it off.)

The following morning my husband Michael had already gone to work when little Michael came into my room. I will never forget it. He had these HUGE crocodile tears that were shooting out of his eyes the way water streams from a squirt gun! I was making my bed and I asked him, "Michael what is going on? What is wrong, honey?"

He tearfully explained, with his hoarse morning voice, "I HAD the tooth this time. Mom, I HAD the tooth! BUT this time the Tooth Fairy didn't leave me any money! I checked!"

He was so sad. Michael never really pouted as a child. But that morning he was clearly disappointed and distraught.

So, just in the snap of my fingers, in a nanosecond really, I began to lie. I mean, it took no creativity whatsoever. Lies were tumbling out of my mouth the way dirt dumps from the back of a dump truck.

I said, "Oh, you're kidding me? Did the Tooth Fairy really forget to take your tooth and leave your money? Michael, I'm SO sorry! Now, you do know that I was a teacher before you were born, so I know how this works. Sometimes, if Mommy had a special meeting or a doctor's appointment or something like that, I would have to send somebody else to teach my class. This is just called a substitute teacher." (Bologna, Bologna, Bologna! BOLOGNA!)

I said, "I am wondering if the Tooth Fairy just needed to be gone somewhere or had another appointment and so SHE had to send a substitute. You know what Michael? The substitute is doing her very best job. I know, because I was a substitute before I got my own classroom of students. Trust me, it's a hard job! The substitute is just trying to do her own thing, but she's just NOT exactly like the regular teacher. So, I betcha the substitute Tooth Fairy just didn't get all the details right or maybe didn't have our home address!" (I'm making up ALL this bologna!)

I continued, "Let me think. Maybe the substitute got confused, so what I'd like for you to do is go back to your room and check again while you finish making your bed. Just check under the bed and around it, not just under your pillow, okay?"

He sniffed, "Okay! Yes, mom."

"Just check one more time. Look down on the floor and look under the bed. Maybe the substitute messed up or got her instructions mixed up and left the money there."

As soon as he left the room, I scrambled around, spinning dizzily, like a top. *Oh, no! What am I gonna do? WHAT am I gonna do?*

What am I gonna do? In our house, little Michael's room was next to ours. I only had a few brief seconds before he'd return. I stood beside the built in shelves near our bedroom door. On these shelves sat some knick-knacks, a few picture frames and a small, ceramic jar where we kept loose change. So, I stared at the coins in the jar in a panic, but I couldn't remember the rate for losing a tooth. Ugh! *I don't know how much to give the kid! I can't remember what dad gave him last time!* I frantically grabbed some coins and dashed off as fast as lightning with my clutched, coin-filled fist, back over to our bed. I shove the coins under my husband MICHAEL'S pillow. (I'm so clever. My husband is Michael AND my son is Michael, too! So, I just tossed them under my husband's pillow.) Meanwhile, my young son checked in his room and came back completely dejected.

He told me his woes in a very Eeyore-like and staccato trembling, voice, "N - no, I checked on the-a-a - FLOOOR! I - I looked under the-a-a bed! N-nope, Mom. No-t-there." Sniff! Sniff!

Then I said, "Rats! Well, honey, I'm so sorry. Maybe the substitute got confused. could you just come help me? Help me make the bed over here. You get on Dad's side." So as he was helping me, I said, "You know what Michael, could you just fluff that pillow a little bit?" (The lies just kept comin' out of my mouth, freely lying to him through my teeth) "Why don't you fluff that pillow a little bit?"

He picked up the pillow and gasped, "MOM! There's a bunch of coins under DAD's pillow!"

I tossed my head back, lifted my eyes upward, right hand raised and nodded as if to signify my 'Ah ha,' moment. I exclaimed through laughter, "Oh, I bet you the substitute just got the wrong

MICHAEL! That's the only thing I can think of! She put the money under Daddy-Michael's pillow. Silly substitute Tooth Fairy!"

Michael was as happy as a clam! He got his cash and he was so excited. The lie had been perpetuated but he was calm and fine.

So, guess what? When Andrew lost his first tooth, our little Michael took him aside to tell him all about the Tooth Fairy. "Now Andrew! I need you to know that when you lose a tooth there could be some mess ups. The Tooth Fairy might send a substitute!" And Michael unknowingly perpetuated the lie!

Why have I gone on and on about this? The reason that my young son Michael believed this lie is that it came from someone he trusted, me! His own mother for goodness sake!

I don't know about you, but I think that we have all accepted, received and believed lies. Sometimes it is because the lie comes from someone we trust: a parent, a spouse, possibly a teacher in your formative years, or a sibling. These lies can cause wounds. These lies can hurt us. It seems ridiculous! Yet, when we willingly accept and believe these lies, they become a part of the fabric of our identity.

Seriously, we can become so off track or confused. Our identity forms around them and our identity may be in crisis rather than in Christ. We may think these lies are the truth. Instead, we need to recognize the lies and reject them. Yet that is not enough because rejecting them leaves a void and more lies can continue to come right back in. So when it comes to lies we must recognize, reject and replace them. Yes, we must replace the lies with truth. We must dwell on God's truth and his promises from Scripture. We must believe the faithfulness of God, His character and His Spirit's voice. We must soak up the things that God tells us in His word. The truth must replace every lie. And strongholds that form because of a lie can be pulled down in the mighty name of Jesus. (2 Corinthians 10:3-5.)

So my question is this. Is your identity in crisis or in Christ?

Whose view do you have of yourself? If it is God's view then it is truth. He says that you are His masterpiece, His Ta Da! His treasured possession. As you sit reading this, perhaps you've had thoughts and voices pop into your mind. Whose voice are you listening to today, right now?

Think carefully about each message and the messenger that brings it. Let's train our ears to hear the Father, God. His voice is the only one that counts. Our spiritual ID bracelet has our name and our Father's name on it. Remember to whom you belong and what He says about you. That is your source of truth and your true identity.

Zephaniah 3:17 The Lord your God is with you, He is mighty to save. He will take great delight in you, He will quiet you with his love, He will rejoice over you with singing.

Ephesians 2:10 For we are God's workmanship, created in Christ Jesus to do good works, which God prepared in advance for us to do.

Psalm 139:13,14 For you created my inmost being; you knit me together in my mothers womb. I praise you because I am fearfully and wonderfully made; Your works are wonderful, I know that full well.

Romans 8:38– 39 For I am convinced that neither death nor life, neither angels nor demons, neither the present nor the future, nor any powers, neither height nor depth, nor anything else in all creation, will be able to separate us from the love of God in Christ Jesus our Lord.

Lily Pads

When you know the truth about who you are and who God is, lies are less readily believed and more easily rejected. Whether it is truth about the Tooth Fairy or anything else for that matter!

Four

Grace's Lost Cell Phone

I received this text from my daughter Grace one morning: "Hi. It's Grace on Christina's phone. I have no idea where my phone is. Maybe I dropped it or left it at home? Would you mind checking in the house/garage?"

That sent my husband Michael, my son Andrew and me into major search mode. We called it to hear it ring and we went through things in her bedroom, bathroom, the entire house, garage and driveway.

Later, when my son Andrew went to class, we asked him, "Please drive slowly and trace her route." We prayed knowing that God is El Roi, the God who sees and not even a sparrow falls to the ground without His notice. Yeah, yeah, that sounds nice, but seriously God sees everything. You cannot hide from Him. He notices everything.

"Are not two sparrows sold for a penny? Yet not one of them will fall to the ground apart from the will of your Father." Matthew 10:29

As we searched, I thought, it's a phone. An expensive phone, yes, yet still, just a phone. We desired to find it. We worked together. We prayed. We regarded it precious. I wanted to find it not only for Grace but for her father who would want her to have it even more than she would. It made me think about these passages of

Scripture in the Gospel of *Luke 15:8-10*

"Or suppose a women has ten silver coins and loses one. Does she not light a lamp, sweep the house and search carefully until she finds it? When she finds it, she calls her friends and neighbors together and says, 'Rejoice with me; I have found my lost coin.' In the same way, I tell you, there is rejoicing in the presence of the angels of God over one sinner who repents."

The previous parable also reminds us of God's love for sinners. *Luke 15: 3-7*

Then Jesus told them this parable: "Suppose one of you has a hundred sheep and loses one of them. Does he not leave the ninety-nine in the open country and go after the lost sheep until he finds it? And when he finds it, he joyfully puts it on his shoulders and goes home. Then he calls his friends and neighbors together and says, 'Rejoice with me; I have found my lost sheep.' I tell you that in the same way there will be more rejoicing in heaven over one sinner who repents than over the ninety-nine righteous persons who do not need to repent."

The whole escapade of the lost cell phone made me reflect. How do I approach the "lost" precious people of the world? Do I want to find them? Or have them be found? Do I work with others, the way my husband and I banded together that morning, as a "search and rescue" team? Do I pray fervently? Am I concerned, even restless, about their state of "lostness?" I have to admit that I don't. Most times, I think of the lost as pretty "okay." I don't need to rock their boat. I have allowed myself to go after lost THINGS more readily than lost PEOPLE.

How about you? Is there anything missing or lost in your life? Are you continuing the search? Let's pray that the lost items or, more importantly, the lost people are found.

Make a list of the people and pray for them.

The LOST is now found! The rest of the story. Here it is: Grace went to the university's parking lot to check near, around and beneath her motorcycle. Apparently, someone found it before she went out to check. That is why she didn't see it anywhere. It was turned in at the University offices. Praise the Lord!

Jesus said he came to seek and save the lost. Lost people can also find God. And we, as his servants, can help them find Him as well.

This short prayer entry is from my journal that morning.

Lord, Thank you that you allowed Grace's phone not to be lost, stolen, crushed or broken, but be found and turned in at the lost and found desk of the office. I praise your name Lord Jesus! You hold all things together by the power of your word. God you see all things, even the sparrow that falls...you notice. You notice the dropped cell phone too! Thank you for Jesus who came to seek and save that which is lost. Help me care about the lost and do any part to make them found. Amen.

Five

"Were You Hurrying?"

My parents, Richard and Lorraine, came for an extended weekend visit. It was a late summer's last hurrah before their grandkids headed back to their respective universities. My folks have upheld this tradition since my oldest began kindergarten. I'm so grateful they are still able to drive the eight hours as they are both octogenarians! We celebrate each new school year by going out to eat at a restaurant chosen by the kids. Selecting the restaurant, time for dining, and all converging, always proves to be a lengthy process, but very worthwhile in the end.

During their visits we also shop, hangout, eat, nap, go thrifting at the local Goodwill and other stores, watch movies, eat popcorn, go out to eat again, attend church, shop, eat Italian gelato, stop at garage sales (that we pass en route to our destinations) and eat some more. Sometimes it's the whole family; sometimes it's just my parents and me. Whoever is willing and available goes with us on these excursions. As my parents describe how we drift from place to place, we just "go wherever the buggy takes us!" I love it! The days evolve and unfold with adventure, laughter and memory making. We seem to go, go, go, then pause like the welcomed rest in a well-composed piece of music. These weekends are packed with activity, but we've learned the rhythm and steps like a well-choreographed dance. It is great fun! I'm worn out the day after they leave and still sorry that they had to go. I think that is a really good barometer of my overall delight.

After running around all day, I wanted to make the most of what God had given. I thought, *why not make it memorable and lovely by eating outside?* The weather was perfect on the last day of their visit. It was just the four of us, my husband, my parents and me. We could finally relax. NO RUSH. That was my vision, desire and expectation.

But as I tried to execute my vision, things broke down.

My parents, my husband and I all had gathered in the kitchen, shortly after arriving home. Everyone sat in their spots. I chopped greens for the salad and my mom husked corn, wiping the silk hairs from cobs and rinsing them in the sink. My husband, Michael and my dad sat at the wooden kitchen table with a lap top open, leaning in with anticipation wondering, *did we get 'good deals' on prized tools purchased moments earlier from a neighborhood garage sale?* As they excitedly compared the online price to the one paid, Michael exclaimed, "YES!"

I prepared the salad: Chop, chop, chop! I felt hurried. There was NO timeline or reason to feel that way. I think I adopted stress. My mind raced, *It's passed lunch time, Rachel. You should get this meal going, People are hungry, hurry, hurry, hurry!* Admittedly, I didn't delegate well. Despite my mom's repeated inquiries, "Is there anything else I can do to help you, Rachel?" I tried to do it ALL myself. I didn't want her slaving away. She'd already helped with the corn on the cob.

Still I wanted to make it memorable, a dining experience. This is the phrase we use when things are different from the norm. I was wound tight. I wanted to make it happen in a hurry. Just like Martha in the Bible story getting ticked off at her sister Mary, I was a little ticked off that Michael wasn't observing my need. (*Couldn't he see me running inside and outside, back and forth?*)

Rather than asking him to put away his laptop and help me, I became frustrated and thought: *stop looking up prices of tools! Don't you see what I'm trying to do?* Michael was "busy" too, but I was giving him the eyes. *Don't you see me running circles around you in this kitchen, while you sit there?*

Finally, we made our way into the beautiful backyard sanctuary. Under the green canvas umbrella, we stood and gazed at the feast before us. We had a summer celebration with bright, colored placemats, fun tableware and tasty garden produce fresh from the farmer's market: sweet corn on the cob, smashed thyme-rosemary topped red potatoes, mixed greens with strawberries and kiwi, roasted garlic vegetables, and more! The full color wheel had exploded on the table. Beautiful! I'm salivating thinking about it. Wow! We all sat down, but the moment I placed my behind in the chair, I remembered the coleslaw that I had made a few days earlier was still in the refrigerator.

So, like a jack-in-the box, I popped right up and I went inside to get it. Hurrying, I tried to open the canning jar, but the lid was tightly sealed. Grunting slightly, I tipped the jar, to get a different angle on it, and changed up my grip so it would open. *GO, GO, GO. Get back out there. They're waiting!*

RATS! I spilled the chilled juices on the counter, down the side of the cabinet and finally onto my legs, feet and floor. Ugh! I quickly wiped up the pungent juices. *Hurry, Hurry, Hurry.* Get back out there! *Hurry, Hurry, Hurry. Sit down, eat and enjoy the meal.*

Then I remembered a question my father always used to ask me when I was young. I could hear his voice, "Were you hurrying?" That question used to tick me off. I hated it. I'd be cradled in a fetal position, rocking back and forth and rubbing my scraped shin bone or blowing on my skinned knee, and he'd ask, "were you hurrying?" Oh, that would frustrate me! Mostly, because he was right. I WAS hurrying. Whenever I was wound up, frantically rushing around I would inevitably get hurt. In this situation, my hurry made everything take longer and the spilled vinegar made me smell like a pickle!

"Were you hurrying?" I often ask myself this question. Hurrying seems like an integral part of an American's lifestyle, right? But does it have to be? Are you always in a rush? I call it the gerbil on a wheel syndrome.

As I reflect back on that day, I wonder, what was I thinking? Did I think I'd get a badge for being superwoman by getting food into people's mouths faster than the local McDonalds? By hurrying, did I miss the offer for my mother's help? Didn't I see that Michael was in his own "zone?" Did I think he could read my mind? Was I experiencing the fruit of the Spirit? Was I practicing *love, joy peace, patience, kindness, gentleness, goodness and self-control? (Galatians 5:22-23)* I ultimately had to ask myself if my hurrying made me more joyful or if it robbed me of my joy.

There are so many things in our life today that cause us to rush and hurry. It could be a job, commute, committee meeting, sporting event, team practice, music lesson, rehearsal, social outing, or a church activity that fills up our day and pushes us to rush around.

When overloaded with commitments we can find ourselves in, what John Ortberg calls the disease: Hurry Sickness. In his book, The Life You've Always Wanted, Ortberg shares advice that a wise friend gave him when he asked for some spiritual direction, "You must ruthlessly eliminate hurry from your life." He later reminded readers, "This does not mean we will never be busy. Jesus often had much to do, but He never did it in a way that severed the life–giving connection between Him and His Father." This a convicting thought for me. Is it for you too?

When my father asked me as a kid, "Were you hurrying?" He may have been trying to teach me to SLOW DOWN or make the correlation between hurry and hurt. Will I get hurt by hurrying? For me, I'd have to answer, yes! I can get hurt physically, emotionally, relationally and even spiritually.

Can we "hurry" relationship? Psalm 46:10 says, *"Be still and know that I am God; I will be exalted in the heavens, I will be exalted in all the earth."* I need to be still and know that he is God. Be still. Know God! I can't get to know Him through hurry. No one gets to know anyone by hurrying the process. There isn't an express lane or drive through window to get to know God. Be still. Know God!

I must look Jesus in the face and see Him in all His glory. Will I sit? Or will I be worried and upset?

"Martha, Martha," the Lord answered, *"you are worried and upset about many things, but only one thing is needed. Mary has chosen what is better, and it will not be taken away from her."* Luke 10:41,42 Sit at Jesus' feet like Mary. Hmm? *Mary has chosen what is better and it will not be taken away from her.* She invested her time and energy into something that couldn't be taken away. I need to do the same thing. Do you?

Will I stop hurrying? Will I sit at the feet of Jesus? Will you? My times of closest intimacy with God have been when I've chosen what is better and I practiced time with God as a consistent rhythm in my life. I have practiced this for years but somehow hurry has a way of creeping back in.

Unchecked, I find myself rushing around like a hamster on its wheel, frantically serving my parents coleslaw on the back deck. I have to remember Mary. I have to choose to be still and know God. I want to invest in the long term. Ultimately, I know that slowing down will benefit me and those around me. And I'm less likely to smell like a pickle!

Six

A Reason a Season or a Lifetime

"*Make new friends, but keep the old, one is silver and the other gold. Make new friends, but keep...*" Do you hear the music? Are you singing along? (It would depend on your age, I guess) As a young girl, I learned this song in music class. It's sung in a round. This simple folk song sums up my friendship experience nicely. The theme of this song runs through my entire life. I've always made new friends and kept the old ones. I like to relate to people and connect with strangers. Like my dad, I'll speak to anyone, but I LOVE making friends much more than merely making acquaintances. The investment pays huge dividends.

People collect many different things. I don't mean to say that people are things but rather we invest in people and gather them around us in the same way. We carry them with us. I think I collect many different people.

On one of his summer road trips, my son Andrew collected a friend named Gabe. Gabe came to stay with us at Christmas time and for a few days in the summer too. One summer morning, Gabe and I were talking about life, faith and relationships. We sat on the back deck and soaked up as much vitamin D as the summer sun provided. We both chomped on a crunchy cereal blend, "You know Mrs. Inouye my uncle always says, 'People come into our lives for a reason, a season or a lifetime.'"

I really liked that perspective: a reason, a season, or a lifetime. It was succinct and it resonated with me. Over the years, I've seen God provide friends for me and I am truly grateful. Some for a reason, many just for a season and others for a lifetime! Or at least so far, I'm not dead yet! I'd like to highlight a couple of gems.

My dear friend Lisa is a southern belle. We met at Grace Church shortly after my move from the Chicagoland area to Minnesota. Immediately I knew, if I got to know her better, we'd be friends. I was given her number for an upcoming church formalized dinner group. I didn't wait. I called for a recipe, or some other silly fictitious reason, just so we could chat.

We were both young moms. She had a traveling husband, a pilot, and I had a husband who worked in retail and often worked late shifts. The friendship was rich. We explored our different backgrounds and discovered our places of common ground. We'd talk about anything and everything and nothing. Our time together included a great deal of laughter because Lisa can turn a phrase! For example, when I asked her if she liked to go camping, she said, "Girl, my idea of being outdoors is to be inside with the windows open!"

Lisa and I spent multiple days and extended evenings together. We both lived close to the Minnesota Zoo, so we'd meet there then let the play continue wherever the day took us. Our children spent many summer nights in the yard playing while we moms made dinner. In my mind, a meal shared together is always better than alone. Afterwards, I'd put my son's pajamas on him and lay him in a play pen while she'd ready her two girls for bed.

We would often pop popcorn and collapse into the couch to watch a "chick flick" together. This routine and rhythm was only the start of hours, even years, of "doing life together." At that time, we had three children between us and now we have fourteen, counting the married children's spouses. Which, of course, I do!

We are doubly blessed because our spouses like each other too! BONUS! The two of us, our children and the men bonded. Our children have strong "growing up together" memories and, in a sense, Lisa and I grew up together too. Our friendship is PURE GOLD.

Lisa possesses the gift of empathy and, as we've lived life together, I've been the receiver more than once. I have a vivid memory of my first miscarriage and Lisa's was the first face to appear at my door. She wondered what I needed and asked how she could help. "Do you want me to take young Michael for you now or is that the last thing you want?" Lisa brought something with her, I believe it was a lush plant in a dark, woven basket, but that is not what stays with me all these years later. I just see her face! It left an indelible mark on me. God sent Lisa. She came. She showed up at my door. It was her presence with me that ushered Jesus' presence in too. She brought encouragement and sweet healing to my sad, mama heart.

Lisa has continued to empathize with me throughout the years. Not long ago, I stood in an Iowa funeral home and I visited with people who came through the line. I was strong. It was my father-in-law Bob's visitation. I loved him. He was easy to love. I knew he loved me back. I felt it. He died five days after a cancer diagnosis. It all happened so fast. A constant line of people streamed through the door and it was a comfort to see how many people loved Bob. But my feet still stung, hot from the continual standing. My back rebelled with a dull ache in the lower section, probably the high heels, and I felt drained. I rubbed my back with the palm of my hand, stretched my neck from side to side and rotated my ankles one at a time. Then, out of the corner of my eye, I saw three of the dearest people on the planet to me. Lisa, her husband and one daughter. I cried. I couldn't believe she'd come. In that moment, I felt so honored and supported. Not until that moment did I realize how much I needed my friend.

Isn't that what God gives us friends for? To love, support, encourage and help us. He gifts us with friends with unique strengths. I have another friend, Stefanie, who is refreshingly honest and reminds me of the Proverb *"an honest answer is like a kiss on the lips" Proverbs 24:26.* She shoots straight and doesn't sugar coat anything. She gets straight to the point. Her thoughts seem to be without clutter and so is her house. Bonus! She is incredibly clean! So, when I clean my house, shuffling piles of paper from one counter to the other, I often think of Stef. What would Stefanie do? I wonder. I have watched her clean her house. If she found "junk," she'd march right over to the garbage and throw it away! She doesn't hem and ha about whether to keep it like I do. She doesn't think of ALL the ways that item could be used, or whether it could be fixed to be functional, or how to repurpose it. No! She throws it away. Maybe that's part of the secret to why she is so clean!

When Michael and I visit the Twin Cities, we often stay at Stefanie and Brian's house. We are so grateful for their long-term friendship and hospitality. One night, while staying in their home, Michael and I crawled into our guest room bed. As I pulled the covers up to my chin, elbows akimbo, I turned my head to the left, looked into his eyes and lamented, "Honey, when we're here at Brian and Stef's, I feel like we're pigs! I mean seriously, the closets in the kids bedrooms are nearly empty, there's no dust in any of the rooms, and everything is in its proper place."

The next morning, I told Stefanie what I had said to Michael. In an attempt to make me feel better she said, "It's clean because we are selling! For last-minute, spontaneous house showings, it needs to be super clean, clutter-free and ready."

As true and comforting as that was, the truth is she's very clean and it's one of her strengths I celebrate. Her cleanliness is a challenge and great reminder for me. But it's easy to be jealous of that strength instead of celebrating it. Jealousy twists up friendship and we end up comparing and competing, especially in the age of Facebook. So I've learned to celebrate her instead of compare myself to her. Stefanie has challenged me with the way she lets God's word stand for itself and I love this dear friend and sister in Christ. I celebrate her and her giftedness. Don't compare. Don't compete. Celebrate!

In friendship, remember this mantra and practice it because it keeps the relationship healthy and encouraging. *Don't compare. Don't compete. Celebrate! Don't compare. Don't compete. Celebrate!* The mantra needs to be repeated and rehearsed because it is so tempting to forget and slip back into the comparison mindset. I encourage you to practice right now. *Don't compare. Don't compete. Celebrate!*

The comparison game is insidious, dangerous and particularly prevalent in the lives of women. When tempted to compare, I use the only antidote available. I rejoice in my friends' giftedness and celebrate them. This encourages them and brings glory to the God who created them. It's a paradigm shift, a conscious choice and deliberate action to celebrate. Instead of feeling small, insignificant or incompetent, feelings that create fertile ground where jealousy likes to wiggle its way in and pollute or destroy the friendship, speak aloud words like "Wow!" Audibly exclaim, "You amaze me!"

When we celebrate one another, we create a safe community where we can belong. And belonging is crucial! God pairs and groups people perfectly together and that's part of His plan. He wants us to connect so that, through friendship and community, He can cause our connected wires to create even more "electricity" for His glory and the Kingdom's advancement. *We, though many, are one body in Christ, and individually members one of another. Having gifts that differ according to the grace given to us, let us use them (Romans 12:5-6 ESV).* Here Paul is describing the church and how our unique strengths combine and complement one another to better everyone.

Comparing and competing steals away the richness of community. But when we celebrate individual's gifts, Lisa's empathy and Stefanie's honesty (and cleanliness) for example, we reap countless benefits. Because of my involvement with friends, my love for God and for others has grown.

My friends have helped shape my understanding of worship and encouraged my devotion to Jesus. And that's how life should be! Whether the friendship is for a reason, a season or a lifetime, we are rich when we connect as friends and do life in community. I know I am rich in friendship because I seem to collect real gems and they're also gold. *"Make new friends, but keep the old, one is silver and the other gold."*

Seven

Presence in the Room

I t was my turn. "Okay, I'm going to see Steve." I said as I left the family waiting room. I walked down the long hallway to Steve's hospital room. As I entered, I reached my hands up to the wall on my right, pushed the button that dispensed hand sanitizer, rubbed my hands together feeling the wetness and coolness of the alcohol over them. *Yup! they're clean*. I sat alone with Steve. Or so I thought.

My brother-in-law Steve was in the hospital because he was very, very sick. He had been ill for a while and wasn't getting better. He was being treated by an infectious disease doctor. Soon after that he had had emergency heart surgery, followed by a coma and finally, his systems all began to shut down. My sister Sharon never wanted him alone. She stayed with him most of the time, but there was always a rotation of willing family members ready to sit by Steve's bedside.

On the edge of my seat I sat on Steve's right, the chair pulled close to his bed. I held his bruised, right hand and stroked it a bit as I chatted with him making sure he knew it was me. I remember taking a stack of ringed Bible verse cards out of my bag and reading them aloud. I'd been meditating on the promises of God for days and I had marked a few that I wanted to share with Steve. I read, *my heart and flesh may fail, but God is the strength of my heart and my portion forever.*

Interestingly, prior to that time I recall the nurses would come in the room at regular intervals and change all the different settings they needed to because all his machines were beeping. Each nurse would check all his lines and tubes and monitors, push a few buttons, then leave abruptly. But not this time. I remember as I was reading God's word, that the nurse just lingered as I prayed and read scripture over Steve. She opened a few more drawers gingerly and looked and adjusted a few things, but became quiet, lingered a few more minutes and left. The sweet Spirit of God in the room was, I believe, why she lingered. It was as if a mist filled the place, but there wasn't any moisture.

I told Steve that I appreciated how he always asked me if I would sing a song for him or even yodel. It seemed like *every* family gathering he'd ask me, "Rach are you going to sing? Do you know how to yodel?" That night, as I sat beside him quietly for a brief moment, the Presence of God filled the room. I don't even know how much he heard me, but I whispered, "Steve, I'm going to just sing over you, okay? So here's a song that's on my heart" I began to sing a Hillsong song:

I will bless the Lord forever
I will trust Him at all times...

As I think back now, I may have thought that I was going to minister to Steve. But it was really the Holy Spirit that ministered to me, well to both of us. As I closed my eyes and sang, I felt the Spirit of God in the room in a very comforting and settling way. I stood and lifted my hands in worship.

Steve really liked music. Although unsure of what one hears while in a coma, my niece Jennifer and her husband, Herb, put some of Steve's favorite songs, including the Beach boys, on an iPod for him to listen to.

I stood there singing and worshipping, but when I finally opened my eyes, I noticed on Steve's LEFT side an earbud from his iPod remained in his ear. There wasn't one in his RIGHT ear, which was the side that was facing me when I first sat beside him. Perplexed, I leaned over Steve's body, took the earbud out, put it to my own and sure enough, I could hear a Beach Boys song playing. I threw my head back, began to chuckle as I listened. Through my laughter I asked "Steve, are you thoroughly confused? I've been singing over you and you've been listening to me and that song all at the same time!"

I just laughed, a bit embarrassed by the awkwardness of the moment. Yet nothing shattered my worship; the music and laughter were a great blend. Oh, how I belly laughed. The kind of laughter that is cleansing because it turned into hot tears that streamed down my cheeks. It seemed those laugh-tears did an extra, well needed, washing of the soul. I know that God is present everywhere, He is an omnipresent God. I also know that He displays His manifest presence at His own prerogative. I feel as though God decided to show Himself so real and tangible in that hospital room. For that, I am forever grateful and will never forget His presence in the room.

Come near to God and he will come near to you. James 4:8a

Cast all your anxiety on him because he cares for you. 1 Peter 5:7

Lily Pads

You make known to me the path of life; In your presence there is fullness of joy; at your right hand are pleasures forevermore. Psalm 16:11 ESV

I'm so grateful I was able to come near to God and experience His presence that day in the hospital room with Steve. I'm grateful I took my turn to sit beside Steve and experience the One who is always beside me. Although I thought I'd be sitting with Steve alone. Being alone was not at all what I experienced.

Eight

Elevators and Chapels

It was a somber day, heavy and tender, but it was a memorable time. It was a gift. My sisters and I were all gathered at Mercy Hospital in Des Moines, Iowa hours before my brother-in-law Steve's imminent death. We wanted to be there for our sister Sharon during these difficult hours. My father Richard had invited us all, along with our immediate families, to gather in the hospital's chapel. We were quite frazzled from the traumatic events of Steve's illness: first a scheduled heart surgery, then emergency heart surgery, a coma and hospital stay. *Remember. Breathe! Take deep, cleansing breaths.* This needed reminder repeatedly looped through my head.

I got into the elevator with my three older sisters, Barb, Sharon and Joyce, and it was just the four of us, no other passengers. Without a word we headed down to the lower level chapel. Our sadness felt like a force. Like an elephant standing on one's chest. My lungs seemed deflated and paralyzed. *Just breathe!*

The mood was somber and weighty. We stood quietly. No movement. We realized no one had pressed the button to go down to the chapel on the lower level. We all looked at Barb because she was closest to it. She extended her hand slowly, pressed the illuminated button, drew back her hand, placed it on her right hip and exclaimed in alarm, "Aw, wait a minute? Oh, no! I think these are my husband Craig's jeans! Seriously?" She pulled at the jeans upper thigh area with both hands as she looked down and she loudly trumpeted, "I think I am wearing CRAIG's jeans. Do these say Lee?"

She swiveled around and thrust her bent fanny my direction. With hip slightly hiked, she rotated her head like an owl, examined the label and asked, "Rach, DO THESE SAY LEE? I don't own any LEE jeans! These ARE Craig's jeans! Oh, Man! Can you believe it? I am wearing my husband's jeans!" (Barb is one of the funniest people I know, but she doesn't mean to be.)

Sharon flung her entire torso against the back of the elevator wall, like a swatted fly. Slowly at first, then quickly she slumped into a crouched position with knees bent. Finally she landed with a plop on the elevator floor. With her head held in both hands, Sharon exclaimed through laughter, "Oh, Barb!"

As she began to laugh, we all joined. We laughed and laughed and gasped and roared uncontrollably! Like a release valve alleviates pressure, this hilarious situation momentarily shattered the sadness. Next, we cried from laughing so hard. Barb, with her silly antics and cluelessness, cracked us up like usual. This struck a welcomed chord. Oh, boy! *Deep breaths! Breathe.* I laughed so hard I could barely breathe. Laughter is good medicine! This was a needed dose... DING!

Elevator doors opened. We were on the lower level. We helped Sharon get up. We all tried to regain our composure. Just a bit farther down the corridor, we opened the door to the quaint beautiful chapel filled with piano music. I noticed my son Michael seated at the piano, voluntarily isolated, in the far corner playing it. We all process difficult things and grief differently. He expressed himself through music. He played every motion picture score he could remember: Lord of the Rings, Pirates of the Caribbean, Star Wars. Beautiful selections from each flowed out of him and into the room. He processed this very difficult time through music.

I wanted my husband near but he was in Wisconsin. I waved my son Michael over and my three children gathered close. My father Richard stood. His voice quivered as he spoke from the front in very hushed tones. He is not usually soft spoken, but this volume level was all he could manage. He thanked God for Steve's life, for the opportunity to know him and to know each other too. His emotions surfaced and his voice cracked a bit. I've witnessed this one other time, years earlier, at my grandmother's funeral, as he spoke of her vibrant life. He loved her.

That same spirit of deep gratitude for Steve's life flooded my Dad's heart, ours and the room. The love and admiration rose like incense rises and floats through space. I didn't want to let Steve go. He's the type of guy who made me feel like I was the most important person on the planet. I had a hunch he made everyone feel that way! I'll never forget this pre-funeral and private family memorial. It was precious. It was needed. It was a gift! So is life!

I remained seated but read Psalm 34 aloud from my red, leather Bible:

The righteous cry out, and the Lord hears them; he delivers them from all their troubles the Lord is close to the brokenhearted and saves those who are crushed in spirit...The LORD redeems his servants; no one will be condemned who takes refuge in him.

Some moments in one's life get paused or "freeze-framed." They are preserved. This sweet time is one of those for me. Although my heart ached that we knew Steve would pass in the next few hours, my heart was also overflowing with thankfulness for him. I experienced grateful grief. This pre-funeral and private family memorial I'll never forget. It was precious. It was needed. It was a gift!

I heard God whisper, *because life is a gift.*

Nine

Worship Leading and Garbage Cans

My twenty minute drive felt endless as I drove home from rehearsal. I was worn out due to the late hour and tired from standing. I turned onto my street and wound around the bend. I saw the entire neighborhood's multiple garbage cans and recycling bins lining its curved street like a child's building blocks. I wondered, *Did my boys remember to take out the garbage and the recyclables?* I hadn't reminded them before rehearsal.

As I drew closer, I discovered our garbage cans positioned between the sidewalk and street. *YAY! They remembered without being reminded!* My proud mama heart was delighted. *Rachel, be sure you thank the boys in the morning.* However, when my headlights illuminated BOTH the cans and the blue recycling bin, my delight quickly changed to disappointment and then disgust.

"Oh no! Oh, man! Yuck!" I exclaimed. One of the two trash cans was tipped over with its contents strewn all over the lawn. I don't know what happened. Maybe the wind knocked the can over. Perhaps a dog or raccoon had reeked havoc. But garbage was ALL OVER THE LAWN! It was so late. I knew my boys would already be in bed and couldn't help me. *Rats!* So, I pulled into the garage and went inside. I quickly found my husband and implored, "Michael, please come outside and help me!"

"Some animal must have come and knocked over the garbage cans, or clawed into the bags, and managed to get garbage ALL OVER THE LAWN! I'm not kidding, it's all over the place!" I repeated my request in that damsel in distress sort of way, "Honey, will you PLEASE come help me?"

All I wanted to do was flop into bed. But, instead, I walked back out to the front yard in the crisp dark night with low, slumped shoulders and reluctantly began to pick up the garbage. I bent down almost in slow motion to gather up gross, smelly, soggy garbage: crumpled up used tissues; slimy banana peels; discolored coffee filters still packed with coffee grounds; pieces from heads of lettuce; apple cores; small bits of plastic torn from the ripped trash liners; cotton balls; and all the typical family refuse.

What makes this all the more problematic is that I have a highly-sensitive, odor-induced GAG reflex! This gag reflex can be so intense that I nearly throw up, vomit, or toss my cookies, whatever you want to call it. When my kids were young, they would observe me sniff the perfume on my wrist when I went into a bathroom that was highly malodorous. Believe me, this wasn't fun as a young mother. Vomit from children even dirty diapers can make my eyes fill with tears, stomach do a flip flop and then I gag!

In the cool of this particular night, with the stars as my light, I tried hard not to gag. So I held a banana peel between my index finger and thumb using them like they were tweezers. With arm stiffly stretched out, I baby stepped sideways, inching my way toward the now righted receptacle. I got just close enough to drop it in. Phew!

Then Michael came to rescue me. It was crisp outside and we could see our breath. He had a snow shovel in his hand. Michael began to shovel the strewn trash from the street, sidewalk and lawn back into the can. I thought his use of the shovel ingenious! There wasn't any snow on the ground but Michael used it to get a lot of garbage collected at one time.

The sound of the metal shovel blade scraped against the concrete and rang out. I was nervous. I thought this activity might wake our neighbor. We made so much noise at nearly midnight. I held my finger to my lips and motioned for Michael to be as quiet as possible! "Shh!"

I don't know how long this process took. I was very tired so it felt like it took forever. Thankful for Michael and glad that the gross, smelly job was finally finished, I trudged up our driveway's slight incline. With arms tightly wrapped around myself, I rubbed them up and down to keep warm. I asked God, *WHY does this kind of stuff happen to me? Are you trying to TEACH me something? Lord, I need to get some sleep! I have to be up early tomorrow to get to church to lead worship.* (Do you ever do that? Inform God of all the things he already knows?)

Then these words impressed my spirit as he spoke. *Rachel, look at the situation. Really look. Don't you see it? Tomorrow, as you lead women in worship, you plan to ask them to reflect on their sin and take time for confession. Yet you often keep your sin contained in a can crammed in with the lid tightly shut so it won't stink or spill out. BUT it's still TRASH. Even when contained in a can. You try to keep the lid on tightly so that no one will see it. BUT I see it. You don't realize to me it is as if the garbage of your life is strewn all over the lawn of your life. This garbage was all over your lawn tonight. You see, I see it! Every bit! Whether in a can or not, it is like that with sin too, I see it! Just confess it.*

Confession? Hmm. I had to ask myself: *Do I even view my sin as sin? Do I quickly confess it? Is it as stinky to me as the smelly garbage on the lawn? Does my sin set off a "gag reflex" in my spiritual life? Why is confession so difficult? Mostly I don't want to humble myself before God or anyone by admitting my failure, my sin, and ask to be forgiven. Perhaps it's pride.* (Ask yourself these same questions.)

Then there is Satan who wants the lid on the garbage can to be kept tightly shut. Satan knows that, IF we confess, God WILL forgive. If we confess we will be restored to complete and full fellowship with God, our Father. Satan can't stand that! He also knows that scripture says, *"Confess your sin to one another and pray for one another that you may be healed." James 5:16* He doesn't want me or you healed.

He wants sin's sick cycle to plague us. Satan wants us to continue to live in the life-sucking, joy-robbing, head-spinning, endless cycle of temptation and failure. During this cycle we experience any one or a combination of things: shame, self-loathing, isolation, pretending perfection, pride, joylessness, stunted growth, depression, denial and the list goes on.

He doesn't want us to admit to anyone that we struggle, wrestle, or fall prey to his tactics. He'd rather keep us repeat offenders and captives than have us recognize the stench of our own sin. He doesn't want us to confess, repent and be free of it. He is the enemy of our souls. Never forget that!

The enemy hates ANYTHING that draws us back to God and confession does that. But sin is SIN. My sin should make me sick. I should gag at its stench before a Holy God. All sin needs to be confessed and forgiven.

But Satan does not want us to recognize sin as sin. He prefers that we keep on believing HIS lies. Lies like:

It's just my personality.

Everybody does this.

No one will know if I just don't tell them.

This is the way ALL women/ many mothers/most Americans are!

You deserve to have this.

Sin? No, not really. This isn't a big deal!

I can handle this.

Rather than confess, we try to keep the lid from coming off and spilling garbage all over. This can be exhausting, right? Yet God sees us and knows all, including the garbage. AND He still loves us. God doesn't just love. God IS love! (There is freedom!)

I had planned to lead a time of confession in the morning as part of the worship set. Visuals make an impact on me and affect me greatly so God often teaches me through them. I believe He thought if it helped me, it might help other women too. Boy, it did.

Absolutely! Nothing is wasted in God's economy. He used even "garbage night" to teach me and the next day I shared this "garbage all over the lawn story" and some Bible verses with the women gathered for worship.

"Come now, let us reason together," says the LORD. "Though your sins are like scarlet, they shall be as white as snow; though they are red as crimson, they shall be like wool." Isaiah 1:18

"If we claim to be without sin, we deceive ourselves and the truth is not in us. If we confess our sins, he is faithful and just and will forgive us our sins and purify us from all unrighteousness." I John 1:8,9

"The Lord is compassionate and gracious, slow to anger, abounding in love. He will not always accuse, nor will he harbor his anger forever; he does not treat us as our sins deserve or repay us according to our iniquities. For as high as the heavens are above the earth, so great is his love for those who fear him; as far as the east is from the west so far has he removed our transgressions from us. As a father has compassion on his children, so the LORD has compassion on those who fear him; for he knows how we are formed, he remembers that we are dust." Psalm 103:8-14

God sees us and knows all, including the garbage AND He still loves us. God doesn't just love. God IS love! Reflect on these scriptures and experience God's love and forgiveness:

"Out of the depths I cry to you, Lord; Lord, hear my voice. Let your ears be attentive to my cry for mercy. If you, Lord, kept a record of sins, Lord, who could stand? But with you there is forgiveness, so that we can, with reverence, serve you." Psalm 130:1-4

"He saved us, not because of righteous things that we had done, but because of his mercy. He saved us through the washing of rebirth and renewal by the Holy Spirit." Titus 3:5

"But God demonstrates his love for us in this: While we were still sinners, Christ died for us." Romans 5:8

"Yet this I call to mind and therefore I have hope: Because of the LORD'S great love we are not consumed, for his compassions never fail. They are new every morning; great is your faithfulness." Lamentations 3:21-23

"Therefore, there is now no condemnation for those who are in Christ Jesus, because through Christ Jesus the law of the Spirit who gives life has set you free from the law of sin and death." Romans 8:1,2

Lily Pad: Back to the garbage on the lawn: The morning after the garbage/lawn episode I did lead women in worship. I'm not sure how many of the above verses I shared but I shared some. We had a time of confession built into the worship song set. I too confessed my sins. I may have confessed my outburst of anger directed at my kids, my judgmental attitude toward others, my pride and desire to be right or get the credit, or my lack of faith in God's concern for my situation. Any number of things could have been what I confessed to him and to the other women in my group that day. I don't really remember.

One thing I do know, God heard my confession. He took that sin or sins and threw them as far as the east is from the west. Those sins are gone and he remembers them NO more! (FREEDOM) Maybe that's why I can't remember them clearly now either. They're GONE! He remembers them NO MORE! Praise His glorious Name! I sure hope you are thankfully waving your imaginary white hanky in the air right now shouting. "Amen! Preach on, sister, preach on! Thank you Jesus!"

God reminded me that he is WAY beyond the best garbage man ever. It is NOT only a once a week garbage/sin removal agreement. I can confess and receive His forgiveness and garbage removal moment by moment. I don't have to pay Him anything for it. Jesus paid it all. Because of Jesus' blood shed on the cross I am forgiven. My sin condition is gone! I may stand faultless before the throne of Grace to obtain the grace and mercy that I so desperately need. The daily sins that I continue to commit against Him, when I confess, He still forgives.

Perhaps you need to take some time right now. Seriously, put this book down and come clean with God. Just call it what it is. Sin. Agree with God about whatever it is. Receive forgiveness right now. God sees all! Just like garbage spread on the lawn. He sees. He knows! He alone can cleanse from ALL unrighteousness. His response to confession is unchanging. If we confess, his response is complete forgiveness and pure love. I plead with you and I remind myself too. Confess. Don't wait for a raccoon to expose it.

Ten

A Walk with Charlie

I'm quite pet-impaired so little did I know I'd learn from God about fear through a dog! One spring day, God prompted me to text my neighbor, Mary, to go out for a walk. I wasn't sure if she'd be available. I'm a bit embarrassed to admit that I didn't act on the Holy Spirit's prompting but went out alone. I approached my final stretch toward home when I saw her coming toward me on the other side of the street with her dog. So I asked, "Are you just starting out? Would it be okay if I joined you?"

"Sure you can join us!" She replied.

Just then her dog came bounding across the street, jumping up at me. His paws dug into my thighs while she chided him "Get down! You know Rachel's not a dog fan. Charlie, get down!" He obeyed.

"You know I almost texted you about an hour ago!" I said.

"Really?" she replied.

I found out why God wanted me to text her hours earlier. It happened to be her birthday! I love that the Holy Spirit had placed her on my heart and in my mind and when I didn't obey, He still gave me a second chance to spend time with her in what seemed like a chance meeting. I was prompted to text Mary earlier, but the enemy of my soul, Satan also tried to discourage my efforts to finish this book earlier that same day. As we walked along, I felt God repeatedly do what I call His show and tell. He wanted to teach me about my walk of faith with Him exposing the enemy and his tactics to use fear to stop me.

We strolled along and she apologized profusely, "I feel like walking with Charlie slows you down Rachel. I'm so sorry!"

I told her, "It's no big deal, Mary. I've already finished a couple of miles of walking and jogging. I'm fine with this pace."

The dog wandered all over the neighbor's lawns. He sniffed here and stopped there as she kept calling him. "Charlie, come on now."

He sniffed a while longer, wagged his tail then joined us. I was very surprised and impressed because at the end of every block her dog sat on the sidewalk and waited to cross the street until my friend tapped or touched his head. That signaled him, "It's okay to go across now."

It was such a beautiful picture of master and canine. He would wait until it was okay for him to proceed, listening to her commands, and with the slightest touch from her, he knew it was ok to move on.

I thought about the things going on in my life that day; publishing this book, career paths for my husband, questions and transitions going on in my kids lives, all of which seemed so foggy. But I know all will be made clearer when needed. I thought about not moving ahead until the Holy Spirit taps me on my head and says, "Okay, move on!"

We reached Madison Street which includes a very steep hill. As we walked up its steep incline and leaned in, my heart began to beat a bit more rapidly, partly from the increased difficulty and partly because of what I knew was ahead. We were approaching a bank of evergreen trees that line the border of one particular property. The property where two dogs dwell: the first an Alaskan Husky that just looks like an Eskimo (just strap a sled behind it!) the second a light gray Schnauzer.

I could hear both dogs barking, even though we had only begun to approach the yard and their view was obscured by the tree line. I'm pretty pet impaired so I turned to Mary and I said, "Those dogs have one of those electric fences, right?"

She assured me "Yes, they do."

We continued marching up the hill.

Recessed but up on the grass on the side of the bank stood the two dogs. The Husky stood like a sentinel guarding the property, his front paws perched on a railroad tie structure encompassing a garden in that property's backyard. He barked and he howled and he growled as the Schnauzer ran up and down along the invisible fence line. The Schnauzer ran, so frenzied, back and forth like a football coach paces during a close game with one more scoring opportunity. Then the Husky moved from his post, while still growling and barking, and charged forward. Then he circled back and charged toward us again, baring his teeth.

Curious as to what he would do, I glanced down at Charlie who was very timidly walking toward that property on the lined sidewalk. He seemed to slow almost to a complete stop. I loved what happened next. Mary extended her hand and stroked Charlie's reddish golden coat as she coaxed him along reassuringly, "It's okay Charlie. C'mon let's keep going!"

Without getting too touched by this visual demonstration of a spiritual truth, I was so pleased to see *God encouraging me through the dog. It's as if God told me: It doesn't matter how much Satan growls or barks or tries to frighten you, if this is the direction I want you to go, I will stroke your back and encourage you to continue on the path. But know that I will walk right beside you.*

I thought that was absolutely precious that the Lord chose to coax me along through my friend coaxing her dog.

As we rounded the corner toward another one of the neighborhood streets, we saw a chain-link fence that contained two dogs. I don't even remember what kind the big one was, but I clearly remember this tiny, black Chihuahua about the size of one of my puffy bedroom slippers. That dog was yappin' and yippin' in such a high-pitched bark that I thought she may explode in the next 20 seconds.19,18,17,16,15! "Bark, bark, bark, bark, bark!"

Charlie, was about 10 times her size and weight but he was so freaked out by that dinky dog's bark. I thought, *Seriously Charlie? You could swallow that little dog the way a snake detaches its hinged-jaw to swallow a mouse in a single gulp! Don't be afraid!*

Mary shook her head and giggled a bit. "I know, I can't believe how frightened he gets of that little tiny yappy thing!"

"Yeah, I can't understand it," I chuckled back.

Yet, I could totally relate. Hours earlier, that same day, my enemy, though so small compared to my BIG AWESOME MIGHTY God, really wanted to make me cower too!

My prayer: Lord, thank you for the lessons I've learned while on my walks, the lessons I've learned looking at dogs and the lessons You desire to teach me. I do not need to be afraid. I know that You go with me. You are never going to leave me or forget about me.

You are the one that instructs me and teaches me in the way I should go. Your counsel watches over me. (Psalm 32:8)

You tell me. *Have I not commanded you to be strong and courageous? Do not be terrified. Do not be discouraged for the Lord your God will be with you wherever you go. (Joshua 1:9)*

So how about you? What is the "little black Chihuahua" that is barking at you and making you think you should stop advancing? What is your "Alaskan Husky" that seems to be ready to charge at you? Know that the Lord, your good Shepherd, is wanting to stroke you on the back and move you forward into his ever increasing good will and plan for your life. I challenge myself and I challenge you to stop, listen to His voice, and wait for a tap on the head indicating, "Let's cross now!"

Let's keep on walking with our Master! He knows your way. He knows mine. He knows your name and mine. He knows your birthday and He knows mine. He knew it was my friend's birthday that day too.

In fact, every day ordained for us is written in His book before any of them come to be. He delights in you and he delights in me. So let's take a walk, without fear, with Him!

Eleven

Bull or Steer?

The Bible is full of simple truths they aren't complicated. I often forget how simple truth can be. My nephew Beau reminded me of how ideas can be so simple but we complicate them. This idea was made clear to me when Beau was young. This skinny, Iowa farm boy was an adorable towhead, complete with a pair of small and slightly smudged, eye glasses. He had dimples on both cheeks and a huge smile on his face as he ran off to the barn ahead of me. He ran excitedly ahead because he wanted to show me his 4-H project. He hollered, "Hey, Aunt Rachel, ya wanna come see my calf?"

So I followed him out to the barn. As I opened the barn door it was cool inside and dimly lit. It took a moment for my eyes to adjust. I smelled the straw as I stepped on it and heard it crunch. As my eyes adjusted, I saw Beau's profile first. He was a bit elevated while climbing the metal gate, his blue jeans pressed up against the rungs that worked as a fence keeping me protected from what I saw next. A HUGE beast!

Yikes! My sweet little nephew is going to lead this beast around the 4H ring at the state fair? For some reason, my mind pictured a 'calf' to be something small. Just a little wobbly, creature wanting to suck milk from its mother. *No, no, no!* I swallowed hard because, there before me, in close proximity I might add, with its flaring nostrils and its hot breath, was a jet black, beast weighing at least ten times what I did. This calf was really, a huge STEER.

Beau continued to tell me about this calf/steer. He told what he does to care for it, how often he feeds it and where he would be showing it. All of those kinds of details. I listened intently, I remember looking at Beau as I asked him a bit embarrassedly, "Beau, what's the difference between a bull and a steer?" Without missing a beat, he cocked his head a bit, as his soft white-blonde hair shifted slightly, looked me directly in the eye, and said, "Oh, Aunt Rachel, a steer is JUST a bull with the seeds taken out of its butt!" Okay! That was clear as crystal to me. Steer. I looked up in the dictionary just now. It reads a castrated bull. Simple NOT complicated, very clear.

God's word is often times as simple, but we complicate it. Maybe it is because we are reluctant or choose not to obey Him. *Blessed is he who listens to these words of mine and obeys them. Matthew 7:24* What does that mean? Well, you don't have to look it up in the greek.

Here are a few more simple truths to ponder:

Be quick to listen, slow to speak and slow to become angry.

Do not be anxious about anything.

Cast all your cares upon him for he cares for you.

Simple! Clear! Uncomplicated! EASY?

Twelve

The Water Level is Rising!

"Sister's Weekend" approached so I excitedly converted my children's bedrooms into guest rooms for my three older sisters which takes more doing than the wave of a simple wand. This particular spring it was easier because our empty nest longed to be occupied.

As their arrival drew nearer, I became extremely excited. What would the days of their long-awaited visit hold? I wasn't sure. We always have so much fun. Once my sisters arrived, we decided on our tentative schedule: local farmer's market, jewelry stores, a delicious lunch (of course) and a stop by a boutique that has some of my friend's items as part of its inventory!

We enjoyed our tasty lunch and we were about to head out to visit the boutique that I knew my sisters would go bonkers over, but when we squinted out the restaurant's window we noticed the people waiting at the crosswalk because their hair was blowing sideways like a waving flag. We commented, "It might be raining. Is it raining? Or are the leaves just blowing around?" All of these a sure sign of a storm. "Is that woman getting wet?" we asked each other. We really couldn't tell. We grabbed our jackets and purses when

Barb inquired, "How far away did you have to park, Rach?" I dropped off my sisters earlier because the air was so humid. (Yes, a sign of a storm.) "I'm just two or three blocks away," I told them. We decided we'd risk it and make a mad dash for the car. We all looked at each other and nodded our heads in agreement. "Let's GO!" we exclaimed.

No one had an umbrella and none of us really knew if it was truly raining or just blowing until we opened the door. Then, in one blast, we all knew because it was clearly "Dorothy and Toto" crazy weather outside. The type where you think you should run around and shout, "Auntie Em, Auntie Em!" like Dorothy from the Wizard of Oz.

We sprinted to the car and ducked intermittently under a few store awnings as we made our way down Main Street. Grateful to have escaped the wind and rain monsters that had chased us ferociously, Sharon and I flung ourselves into the front seats of the car. We sat panting for a moment and were soaked. We looked out the front windshield to see Joyce and Barb still underneath an awning. We hoped it would let up. Barb held her jacket above her head to form an umbrella, but the rain poured over her like a faucet turned to full blast. I reached behind to open the back passenger car door a crack so they could easily enter when they decided to make a run for it. Phew! They made it safely inside.

We all screamed, "BURR!" We were so chilled and drenched. I turned on the heater and the defroster full blast as we shook our heads like wet hounds. We tried to fluff our hair, but it was plastered to our heads. My hair usually has so much hair product in it that I knew it was a lost cause. It had already turned to glue as I feared! We each shed our soaked outer layers. I traveled the most direct path I knew toward our planned destination. The windshield wipers were set on the swiftest setting and the sound of the rain hitting the metal roof was nearly deafening.   So I basically screamed my inquiry so they'd hear, "DO we STILL WANT to go over to the shop where my friend sells her things?" As I approached the road for the turn the rain turned too. It turned into a torrential downpour! Seriously, we nearly needed an ark. Just call me Noah!

I peered up the hill, the road ahead looked like a waterfall. White water spilled rapidly down. It didn't appear passable, unless by boat. So my sister Barb instructed in her determined legato voice, "RACH, we better just STOP along the side of this road. Really, Rach, we should probably just PULL OVER!" Sharon agreed and directed me to a spot she had spied out the passenger-side window. Beneath the sweeping branches of a weeping willow tree, we sat and waited. We giggled and gasped as we watched the water streaming down the window like we were going through an automatic car wash.

"Oh, my, my, my, merciful heavens!" Barb was chanting! We all looked like drowned rats and we still shivered from our cold dash to the car. The heater was blowing which helped a bit but it made the windows fog over; trading one problem for another. "Oh, my, my, this is quite a DELUGE!" Barb kept saying. "Oh, my, my, my this IS a deluge! Oh my, my, my merciful heavens!" We waited there awhile. We began to travel up the steep hill slowly. I didn't want the car engine to stall.

When our hopes of shopping at the long awaited boutique were nearly washed away, the rain momentarily stopped, so we pressed on. We crept down the street at about 5 mph where sections of the road dipped causing the rain to pool. Because the pouring rain had fallen so quickly and hard, there was no way for the water to run into the sewers and drain fast enough so they backed up and bubbled over looking like a fresh water spring. As the water level rose we sat by the traffic light trying to decide whether or not we should continue. We waited an entire green light, yellow light, red light cycle debating. GREEN LIGHT! We decided to continue on toward our desired destination.

As I looked ahead, we started to creep along the street that lead to the interstate. Some drivers wisely turned around to avoid the flooded street while others pulled off into a parking lot that lined the road. The water level had risen too high to proceed safely, so I pulled in the parking lot too. One determined traveler continued down the street toward us. As the gentleman's small vehicle approached, it completely stalled in the middle of the road. "Oh, my! This is a deluge!" Barb exclaimed again as the water level rose and was halfway up his driver's door. "Look at that guy!"

We also spied police cars stopped while officers set up orange and white blockades in the street to prevent additional travelers from the same peril while other road blocks floated by and bobbed along down the street, like bath toys. One police officer waded into the deep flood waters to retrieve them and pulled them to higher ground.

After this second delay, I was relieved as I looked up at the sky. It was clearer and bluer in the direction of the long awaited store's location. We finally reached it and had a splendid time. I'm sure we helped to raise the shop's daily sales. My, my, my, merciful heavens I won't soon forget that day's rain or its water levels. It was, like Barb said, a DELUGE!

The street that day was like a river which reminded me of a Bible passage from Ezekiel. Let me include a portion of Ezekiel 47 as you look at the increasing depth of the river, rejoice in the river of God's love and grace in your life if you know Him as the Lord and Savior of your life, then thank Him too.

Ezekiel 47:1-12 *The man brought me back to the entrance to the temple, and I saw water coming out from under the threshold of the temple toward the east (for the temple faced east). The water was coming down from under the south side of the temple, south of the altar. He then brought me out through the north gate and led me around the outside to the outer gate facing east, and the water was trickling from the south side.*

As the man went eastward with a measuring line in his hand, he measured off a thousand cubits and then led me through water that was ankle-deep. *He measured off another thousand cubits and led me through water that was knee-deep. He measured off another thousand and led me through water that was up to the waist. He measured off another thousand, but now it was a river that I could not cross, because the water had risen and was deep enough to swim in—a river that no one could cross. He asked me, "Son of man, do you see this?"*

The river's water level starts out as a shallow trickle and gets ever increasingly deeper. A devotional I read once reminded me that these waters symbolize our continued walk with the Lord. As we believers come to experience more and more of God's all-sufficient power, His ever flowing grace, abundant love and continual provision, we come to realize that His supply for all our needs has NO LIMIT.

As I type this today I still need that truth cemented in my mind. God is not limited. God is awesome in power. He is an all-sufficient God. He has no needs. God is the God who holds the sands of all the seashores in little buckets and weighs the mountains on scales. God is the one who is a star-breathing God. His voice twists the oaks. And mountains melt like wax before Him.

God, thank you that Your love for me has never changed, but as I have walked with You for years my own awareness and appreciation of that love has made me see its great depth and helped me to rest fully in Your goodness and Your provision for me. Thank you for my sisters, thank you for the DOWNPOUR... Thanks that Your love pours down on us too. Help me to float down the river of Your love for me.

Thirteen

"Kratch Back?"

"Kratch back, Dad?" A friend's adorable daughter would ask to have her back scratched often. When she was very young and couldn't quite pronounce the words to her request, but could still be understood clearly, she'd sit directly in front of her father, hunch over and pull her shirt away to welcome his hand on her skin to scratch it. This phrase was quickly adopted by my daughter Grace. Even in her late teen years she'd ask, "Kratch back, Mom?"

One night my husband was gone on a business trip in Chicago. So I asked Grace if she wanted to come sleep on Dad's side of the bed. She crawled into bed late that night or very early that morning, I'm not sure which. I was so out of it, but she slept on his side. I woke to this precious sight. Grace beside me, her long, dark brown hair falling softly across the pillow, spread thick and flat like a horse's mane. Her black Build-A-Bear teddy, Anthony, was almost attached to her shoulder and her blanket was tucked underneath her chin.

I lay quietly on my left side just listening to her breathe rhythmically. As I gazed over at her I began to weep, slowly at first then the hot tears flowing, stinging my eyes and strangely making my ears feel plugged. A few tears dripped onto my pillow while others ran their course downward, pooling in my ear. I am a big proponent of capturing life, of just trying to drink in each moment because life is a vapor, and it appears for a little while then vanishes away. I was aware of taking a picture of this moment to "freeze frame" it in my mind. I let it sit there and etch its way into my heart. I do try to drink life in and appreciate the present. I was aware of the fleeting moments particularly at that time because in just a few weeks she would head to Michigan to begin her second year of college, but her first year away from home.

Memories flooded my thoughts as I lay there silently, not wanting to wake her. I remembered other mornings when she would find me seated on the couch with my Bible open, like clockwork, she appeared. She would stand like a frozen flag pole at first, a zombie still half-asleep, but then she would sidle in next to me on the couch, swing her hair away and sink her head into my lap. Then she melted there.

I'd stroke her hair and comb my fingers through it. This created a brown nest of hair to vacuum later. I would rub her head and scratch her back until my hand cramped and my fingers began to tingle. As her hair untangled and became smooth as silk between my fingers, she'd often hum to express her delight and appreciation. She loved it! I loved it too! This was our regular morning routine. I would continue to read as I scratched her back. Then, as if I were keeping her, she would turn and say, "I have to get in the shower!" Sweet preserved memories!

That morning, as I watched her sleep, these were some of my thoughts:

Soon I won't hear Grace emerge from her bedroom to come sprawl across me. I won't watch her make the familiar motion that says, please scratch my back. This saddens me. I know she will get up and eat breakfast before her classes start. I know she will greet each professor with a smile. I know she will bless those around her with her fun personality. These things I know because I know Grace. Yet, I wonder, will she know that I miss her dearly?

Last night, as she crawled into bed, I must not have been as out of it as I thought because I recall her telling me the reason she had come to bed so late. She too had been crying. She had been lamenting the upcoming year's changes to her relationship with her boyfriend. She was processing how different it will be. Processing through tears. We all must process change and transition. As she mentioned their late night conversation, my initial thought was - you have NO idea how different! WE have no idea how much change there will be. BUT I'm so grateful for an unchanging God. He is the same yesterday, today and tomorrow. Unchanging in His love for me and for my sweet daughter Grace.

I want to thank God for time with Grace. What a privilege it is to be her mom. Every day has been a gift. She has been a constant source of love and encouragement to me. I have huge folders full of expressions of her love saved; I have many letters, notes, Crayola drawings and Post-It notes stashed away. Ever since she was first able to draw and write her thoughts she has given them to me.

I'm thankful for the years that God has given me to raise her. I thank him for all of our mornings together and breakfasts eaten, perched on barstools at the bar in our kitchen. I thank him for the time spent upstairs seated in comfy chairs with her growing legs dangling over the arm of the chair and cup of coffee in her hands. This image of her will always be tucked inside this mommy's heart.

We communed together with our Bibles open as we read the Word or discussed what we had read recently.

I thank God for all the time we spent in prayer. We prayed about things that made us glad; we prayed about things that weighed us down. We prayed together about the simple and complicated things. We prayed about the drama of relationships in general and for those who are grieving. We prayed for those around us and far away, for strangers and for people that we know and love. We regularly prayed for friends who had gone away to college. Because of these rhythms and routines, I'm sure she knows that I will be praying for her too.

But as I watched her that morning, I wondered. Does she feel the heaviness of my full heart? A heart so saturated with love that the only way to lighten it is to wring it out like a sponge? I suppose that was the purpose of my tears. Those tears were like the release valve of my grateful heart, the wringing out of my heart's soaked sponge. I often say I'm so blessed, happy, or grateful that I'm leaking. I cry because I am so blessed. I will have summers with Grace, Lord willing. I will have spring breaks and Christmas vacations too. I desire to embrace each day and be thankful. That's why I'm thankful that this morning I got to scratch her back, massage her head and stroke her hair as she lay beside me on her Dad's side of the bed. Totally unaware of my weeping. I'm grateful for all the time that I've spent with her. But if I just look back and remain there, it can make me sad. I need to look forward in faith in the ways that God will provide for and protect her. He will grow her fully into the woman that He designed. When I look forward in anticipation, I see her coming back from the university, bubbling over with new stories and experiences and the many joys of things to come that I believe by faith will happen. Then I am encouraged rather than saddened.

This is my prayer of thanks: *Oh God you are good. You know my way and You know Grace's too. Help this mama heart of mine as I transition. Comfort me when I'm sad and lonely. Remind me of all the things that You're doing while she is away. I know that she's never away from You or Your constant care.* The eyes of the Lord are on the righteous and his ear is attentive to their cry. *Thanks that You always hear me when I cry out to You, God. You hear Grace's cries too. Thank you that You instruct her and teach her in the way she should go. You counsel and watch over her. Thank you for the promise that she will go out with joy and be led forth with peace. I love You, God. Thank you for the opportunity to also love her.*

So much has changed since I wrote this chapter. (Publishing a book takes awhile!) But, no matter what happens, my prayer of thanksgiving remains the same. I know God is still in control of Grace's life.

James 5:16b *The prayer of a righteous person is powerful and effective.*

Fourteen

Truth for a Mother's Heart

One morning, while my children were away at college, I began to doubt my role in their life preparation. I was in a real funk and believed that my part in preparing them wasn't adequate. These doubts plagued me from out of nowhere and I couldn't seem to shake them.

What happens when they are faced with temptation or trials? Did you even talk about all the pressures they'd face? A good mom would... These lies swarmed around me like bees around a hive. I felt so many negative thoughts about my children's future. Perhaps you or someone you know can relate?

Whoa! What is this all about? Where is this coming from? I began asking myself. It was an attack from the enemy of my soul, Satan. He tried to rob me of my joy and peace. I did what I know to do when under attack. I went straight to the Word of God and prayed. *Rachel, rehearse TRUTH. It's vital when lies from the enemy come in like a flood because the Lord will raise up a standard against him.* After reading the Word and rehearsing promises of God, I located my "listening journal," a place where I record what I hear God saying to my heart.

I was relieved, even comforted, because before I began to write that day, I flipped back a page or two and reread a previous entry. I don't know why I flipped back those few pages, but my Father's words were FRESH for that very moment. God had already armed me for THIS day. He had spoken truth to combat these lies and this present attack. Here is the journal entry:

(I start each entry with something like this first part) The Lord says my daughter, my love... *Don't be downcast. Come to me, draw near to me and I will give you the desires of your heart. I am well able to direct the path of your life as well as the paths of your children. You need to release them to me. Fully, without doubting that they will be okay. I am their way maker.*

I am the one who began the good work in them—I am faithful to complete it. Do not grow weary in doing well. For you will reap a harvest if you don't give up. Please don't give up. I need you in this army of mine. No one is perfect. Stop trying to manage your reputation or your expectations for your family to be IDEAL. You are a family comprised of sinners. Sinners saved by my amazing grace. You are not perfect, but my love is. You are not kind all of the time, but I am. You are not always quick to forgive, but I ALWAYS forgive.

Come to me. Do you trust me? Draw close. Let me fill you. Do not need or be swayed by the world's empty praises, acceptance, things or possessions. None of that matters or satisfies. I am your ROCK eternal. Will you come to me? Will you stop this cycle of of self-doubt? You think you haven't always been a good mother. You have tried your best my sweet child. You have worked hard and labored well. Be pleased to watch me work out my plans for your children's lives. Lift them up to me. I am the good shepherd. I lay my life down for my sheep. I will keep in perfect peace him whose mind is steadfast because he trusts in me.

WOW! I am so thankful I had logged that in my journal. Even now I can hardly stand it! All I can do is respond with this prayer: *THANK YOU Jesus! This was true the day I heard you speak it to me, the day I reread what you had said and it is still true today!*

Thank you for the encouragement you have given me to keep going because you are the one who completes what you start. I'm grateful. In Jesus name, Amen.

So let me ask you a question. What are the lies you battle against right now? Take a moment to consider their source and recognize them as lies. Do you feel condemned? Do you feel accused? Recognize the voice of the accuser who always wants to condemn you. Reject this voice and the accusing chatter, but don't stop there! Replace his lies with the truth from God's Word. Maybe you'll even write some of the truth in a journal. What's most important is that you have a way to remember truth, God's truth, when Satan's lies attack. Because, as we should all know and remember, the truth will set you FREE!

I shared the day I was in such a funk about my children's future with you so that you can be sure of this, a voice of condemnation and accusation is not from God. When lies come in combat them with truth. We all need to rehearse truth. That's is the only way I got out of my downward spiral that day. Yet this I call to mind, Scripture says, therefore I have hope. We have to call things to mind and we must think about what we think about. I guess that is why we are challenged to renew our minds.

Lily Pads

Ephesians 4:22-24 *You were taught, with regard to your former way of life, to put off your old self, which is being corrupted by its deceitful desires; to be made new in the attitude of your minds; and to put on the new self, created to be like God in true righteousness and holiness.*

2 Corinthians 4:16 *Therefore we do not lose heart. Though outwardly we are wasting away, yet inwardly we are being renewed day by day.*

Fifteen

From Life's First Look to Down on One Knee

I hurried to the top of the steps because they called my name as they entered the house. "Hey, Mom!" As I glanced down to the lower level, Amy turned slowly, caught my gaze and beamed her typical Amy smile. Her hair fell beside her face in soft curls. The bright pink of her dress made her milky, smooth skin have a slight summer glow. She looked absolutely stunning! I said, "Wow! Amy, you look gorgeous." I then turned to Michael and joked, "Hey, Michael you need to take it up a notch. Look at your date! Seriously, you better shower and get ready."

He laughed and sheepishly said, "I know, that's why we've come back. I'm already showered, but I've got to change my clothes." He hunted for the right pants for a few minutes and then emerged from his bedroom, quite dapper himself. He asked me for a bag to wrap the gift he planned to give her. I made Amy keep her distance while he selected the right-sized gift bag and some tissue paper for concealing it.

She questioned, in a high pitched voice, "What is it?" I replied, "I know! I want to snoop it out too." Just before walking out the door, he whispered a few final instructions to me for later. (I was clued in on most of his plan but my heart was delighted and pounding.)

When they returned from dinner, Grace was supposed to take a few photos of them. Hopefully, Amy would just think it was a planned photo shoot to celebrate their dating anniversary. I know Michael planned to go to the same location where he first declared his interest in dating Amy. Three years ago that day! Oh, how time flies. That was the plan, but we would see because it had rained moments ago and I still heard some distant thunder. If his plan worked, he intended to drop down on one knee and propose to her! So surreal! He would be down on one knee, his low position meaning that he will have to look up into her eyes, look at her, express himself and declare his love for her. He will look up into her eyes. That thought takes me back over twenty-three years.

I'm tearing up as I write. Perhaps one of my most vivid life memories, I now recall the way that he looked up into MY eyes as the OB nurse first placed him in my arms. That moment is forever cemented in my memory. He was wrapped tightly in a white, cotton hospital blanket and was such an incredible bundle. A gift from God. A baby boy! Michael Heggen Inouye, my son. As he peered into my eyes with his black ones, he literally melted my heart. His eyes bore a hole into my mommy's heart that is so deep I still don't truly know its depths. BUT I know it is super deep. I love him so much it is hard to express.

In just a few hours he would look up into Amy's eyes. Those eyes of his had already made a way into her precious heart. Man, I am so thankful for him. I am so thankful for her too. *Thank you Lord Jesus. I have prayed for Michael all his life and I have prayed for the one who will become his wife. This day too will be forever cemented in my memory!*

By the way, she said, "Yes!" and they were married the following summer.

He who finds a wife finds what is good and receives favor from the LORD. Proverbs 18:22

<u>Sixteen</u>

Starbucks

One day, I met a friend at Starbucks. We sat and caught up quickly before another mutual friend arrived for a more formal planning session. When our third member arrived, I hugged her in my normal way. We giggled and chatted standing near our table for a moment, then we all three stepped up to the counter to order our drinks. I let my friends order first.

Because I'd already had a cup of coffee earlier, I wasn't really in the mood for another. I thought something fruity would be the ticket! So I asked the young woman waiting on us, "Do you know if your smoothies are made from the same mix as the Vivano you used to have here? I know it's high maintenance, but I'm not really in the mood for coffee and I try not to have high fructose corn syrup. Vivanos didn't have it in them. That was my cold fruity go to. Now I'm wondering what's in your Starbuck's smoothies?"

Quick question deserves a quick answer, you'd think, but my simple inquiry occurred at the precise moment that the grinding of the coffee did. This caused the machines to blare and hum directly behind my sweet order taker. She looked so confused and she nearly shouted, "I'm so sorry, I can't hear your question! Do you mind repeating it?" The grinding noise stopped. Phew! So, I repeated my question. "I used to order the Starbuck's fruit drinks called a Vivano." No sooner did I get that much repeated when the machines began grinding again. This time I projected loudly as I simultaneously pointed up at the menu board on the wall above her head and said, "Your sign says smoothies. Do you know if your smoothies contain high fructose corn syrup? The drink called 'Vivano' which you used to sell didn't so I used to order that! Could you check about the smoothie for me?" She still looked utterly confused because the noisy machine had resumed grinding and humming again preventing her from clearly hearing me. She leaned in toward me, like she was going to do a standing push-up with both hands on the stainless steel countertop, and she spoke up a bit, "Well, I don't know. I'm not really sure, I'm a bit new here. Besides I can't really hear you." I finally replied, "Oh, just forget it. It's okay, I'll just order a different drink."

I turned and motioned to my friends, pantomiming because it was still too loud to hear me speak. I nodded my head in the direction of the bathroom and smiled, indicating that I was going to use it. I did an about face and headed to the restroom while my drink was being made. As I walked to the back of the shop, the volume level of the relentless noise slowly began to fade. With my increased distance, I noticed, surprisingly, that I could hear the sound of my shoe's heels clicking along the stone floor. Am I beginning to hear?

I entered the bathroom and closed the door, CLICK! Yes, I could hear the lock as it turned. I was so relieved to be out of the deafening hum. I took a deep breath in and exhaled slowly. As I breathed deeply, I heard God speaking to me about how I have so much noise and activity blaring in my life that I have become like the young order taker behind the counter who couldn't hear me question her.

God, are you asking me questions? I thought my prayer. *Are you*

desperately trying to get my attention? Please, please don't give up and say like I did, Oh, forget it. I do want to hear from you now and always!

I often have to ask myself: What are the blaring noises in my life that prevent me from hearing God when He is speaking? Is it constant activity, busyness, music, social media or the grinding noise of the accuser? Is it ever my own voice that is constantly babbling on telling Him in prayer rather than listening to Him speak-also called prayer? Let me mention that listening is quite important. The other stuff that I get so used to rattling on about, He already knows and has a perfect, all wise plan in place to take care of it and in His perfect timing too.

Jesus is our model, right? He often removed himself, went to a quiet place and prayed. He retreated from the crowds and got up early in the morning to be with His Father. If that was His mode for prayer both speaking and listening why wouldn't we follow His example too? His disciples were with him and, although He was a great teacher, healer and miracle worker, what they asked of Him was teach us to pray. That's the thing that they saw Him do and wanted to learn how to do.

So, I gotta ask you the question that hung in my head that day. Is there too much NOISE in your life? What do you need to turn off. What vies for your attention? What do you need to do to hear from God? What do you need to do to hear in prayer?

One thing I know for sure is I/we have to be in the Word of God to even know about Him and certainly to hear from Him. I have to let the Word wash over me as He speaks through it to me.

Happy reading the Word! Happy having it soak in. And as you listen, I hope you can turn the volume dial of life DOWN a bit as you turn UP the volume of His voice. Listen to His voice, He speaks! My sheep hear my voice Jesus said.

Spend some quiet time listening to God's voice. Let Him speak His utter delight in you and love over you now.

Seventeen

Stents for a Birthday Present?

If you could choose any birthday surprise, a get-away, excursion, adventure or present, what would it be? Hmm? I'm not really sure what I would choose. But one memorable birthday present I received a few years ago was a trip to the doctor's office, testing lab, cardiac wing, surgical waiting room, accompanied with coffee from the cafeteria and a night's stay on a stiff recliner in my husband's hospital room. Wow! This was one surprise. A wonderfully expensive yet sovereignly planned and perfectly timed birthday present.

Looking back now, my journal entry was very helpful, even prophetically interesting, two days before that birthday. The following is an excerpt from my journal before my birthday in 2011, a day when I was scared to give everything to God and leave it in His capable hands.

God, I desire to completely follow You. - I pray that You would work in me all that needs to be there for me to fully do that. I pray that I wouldn't love anything more than You; not my parents, not my children, not even my husband. I so desperately want to trust You fully with my life. You have good things planned for me. You love me very much. You delight to give me good gifts. Help me overcome this mindset and fear that if I give You everything You will TAKE IT!

Instead help me see that You don't take everything from me- rather you keep it safe and You guard it all in Your huge, sovereign, powerful hands. I choose to release my parents, children, husband, dreams, health and friends into Your care; You are better able to handle it all than I am. Please stay right beside me. Please give me strength and hope for my future. Please help me not be anxious about the day Michael has his stress test. Please cover me with joy and bless me with a peace that passes all understanding. I ask this, in Jesus' name. Amen.

Psalm 138:7,8 Though I walk in the midst of trouble, you preserve my life; you stretch out your hand against the anger of my foes, with your right hand you save me. The Lord will fulfill his purpose for me. Your love, O Lord endures forever–do not abandon the works of your hands.

Little did I know that just two days later I would receive quite a surprising birthday present. My husband had a stress test planned which I was feeling stressed about. (ironic, huh?) Here's a peek into that stressing and testing day:

November 16, 2011.

At 8:20 Michael and I headed out for his stress test and EKG and echo for his heart. His chest hurt whenever he would exercise. He first felt it while walking on the Great Wall with my nephew, Grant, and his wife, Victoria, in China. He thought he was just out of shape. But at the end of October, we walked around the neighborhood and he felt pain in his heart and arms. He even needed to sit down after he dug a hole in the backyard to plant a mum I'd asked him to plant. Michael had an annual physical scheduled in a few days so he talked me into just discussing his options with his doctor then.

During the scheduled stress test, Michael wanted me to come in with him, but I told him they wouldn't let me. He asked, but the nurse said, "No, she should just wait right here in the waiting area until you are finished."

I waited. But he flunked. His heart was showing signs of blockage at about three minutes into the test – yet they asked if he could keep going so they allowed him to continue for 10 minutes. The nurse came out and got me. "You need to come in, follow me!" The doctor told us he was 90 to 95% sure that there was blockage and he wanted to send Michael to Waukesha Memorial Hospital to get a heart catheter to check it out. He said we could go by ambulance or I could drive, but that we needed to go NOW!

So I drove him to the hospital while he made a few calls to his mom and his sister, Susan. I called my parents too before we arrived at the hospital. Michael was hilarious; he wouldn't sit in the hospital bed for long! He got up often and even fixed the small round table in the room that needed leveling. I scolded him, "Michael you should just sit down on the bed!" I texted our pastors while Michael texted some men from our prayer group.

Pastor Dave visited. He prayed for us and I cried. He left. Then, like a drama where actors enter and exit the stage on cue, our friend Nancy called. I filled her in on the day's unexpected turn of events. She helped us so much and brought a sack lunch for us. She stopped by our house and picked up a few things which included our much needed phone chargers and when she arrived at the hospital, we all plugged in. Just part of God's good timing. Michael, Nancy and I were all on our phones when Pastor Steve walked in and he chuckled at the sight of the three of us on our phones (a sign of the times, I guess). He stayed and visited awhile, shared funny heart related stories and prayed for us and we were grateful.

Donnie, a dear friend, stopped too. His stories always make us laugh. He also had a few heart patient tales to tell. It seems that heart related stories are common with men like baby birth stories are with women. As Donnie prayed for Michael, I grabbed a few tissues because when Donnie cries, so do I. He left just about the time the surgery/or heart catheter procedure was scheduled. The doctor came and introduced himself, asked Michael a few questions about his symptoms and explained a few things about the procedure that he would probably perform based on what he saw and then he exited. All part of God's masterful timing.

Next someone came with the bed to wheel Michael down for the procedure. I gave Michael a kiss outside the room and they whisked him away.

I texted a few more family members and friends to both inform and update them, knowing they would pray. As I sat with Nancy, in the cardiac waiting area, a woman in blue scrubs appeared and explained that they found 99%, 80%, and 60% blockages in Michael's Circumflex Artery with two other blockages of 20% – 30% in the other arteries. She said they would place two stents, one to cover the most severe blockage and another longer stent to span both of the other blockages. As she was about to leave to go back in the room with Michael, I stopped her momentarily, and said, "Please tell him he's REALLY CUTE and he has a good heart!" She grinned and assured me he'd get the message.

Because Michael was fully awake during the whole procedure, he was able to watch the dye being injected into his heart. Nancy and I prayed. I was able to keep it together until I prayed. I cried as I cried out to God. I have come to appreciate my tears that I offer as I CRY OUT to the

Lord. Scripture assures me and I know He hears my cries and keeps my tears in a bottle.

The day never slowed. Each minute was full, rich, purposeful and divinely timed. Waiting for your husband to get out of surgery can be overwhelming and scary but I was blessed with friends who came to visit. There was never a moment that I felt alone. My friend Jill, who works at the hospital stopped by. As we sat, Doris, the volunteer for the ICU waiting area, came over and said goodbye to me. She just wanted to tell me that she hoped everything would work out fine for me and for my husband, Michael – Sweet! God ordained meeting!

After they told me Michael was finished, his cardiologist came and met with Jill, Nancy and me in a conference room. He was kind as he explained what was done, but firm about Michael's situation. He said, "He cannot go on like this! Something's gotta change!" He mentioned Michael not going back to work for 7–10 days, and I thought – OH BOY (Michael is somewhat of a workaholic). Next, the doctor invited us to look at the video footage of Michael's heart. It was taken during the procedure. Wow! Now, that's quite a movie!

He told us to go upstairs where Michael was waiting. When we arrived, he was being hooked up to two monitors. He was awake, but had a slight headache. He had to lie flat for 2 1/2 hours to make sure the femoral artery had no pressure placed on it. Lay flat, no bending the legs, or lifting the head.

Andrew arrived after class and he helped Michael when he was finally allowed to rise. Jill and Nancy left and soon after Dave and June arrived with a bag of carrots for Michael's new diet.

Our friends Shanthini and Vinod came with a yummy dinner that Andrew and I both ate. It was a wonderful "birthday dinner." We visited with another friend who we recognized and we realized that her husband was in the room adjacent to Michael's. Pastor Brandon stopped in to see us too. Each visitor cycled through in a special ordained way.

Then everyone left, including Andrew who had gone to a video shoot. I stepped out of the room to phone people about Michael's progress. God used his people to remind me that He is always there. When I returned I found Michael asleep and discovered my dear friend Elizabeth writing me a note because she thought she had missed me. But again, it was God's perfect timing.

The night was getting late and the room darkened, while we chatted and prayed. She held my hand the way she always does. She brought a fun balloon with fruit on it and a sharpie marker message reading, "Welcome to your new dietary lifestyle! Love you!" It was good to have my sweet friend with me! God wrapped my birthday in His personal loving wrapping paper from morning to night.

Andrew returned and hung out with me. I was tired and emotionally drained. I cried on his shoulder sitting on the couch as we crunched on pretzel sticks that Nancy had brought so many hours earlier. The little lunch she brought fed Andrew, Michael and me.

Andrew planned to go home to work on homework, but he fell asleep instead on the hospital couch/bed. I was thankful for the company. So I tried to get comfortable in the recliner chair, but only got a few hours sleep. Michael was out! In the morning, he woke, ordered breakfast, then Mike, an elder from our church stopped by and checked in on him. He remained as the doctor walked in. As it turned out, he and the doctor knew each other so they got caught up on each others' lives. Another cool God moment! A few minutes earlier or later and they wouldn't have reconnected. You can't script that kind of stuff. All the peoples' entrances and exits and connections totally amazed me.

The doctor told Michael he did NOT want him to return to work right away. "I want you to push a 'reset button,' evaluate and reflect on what is important." The doctor mentioned, "I know because I just returned to work on Monday after being away due to my own heart attack and stent procedure." He admitted, "I didn't want to tell you that yesterday, but it's true and it's made me think! Michael you are young and you need to take this seriously!"

A few minutes later, our dear friend Shanthini brought a breakfast of orange juice and muffins and helped us with our hospital exit strategy. The rehab nurse and the dietitian stopped in while she was there so an additional set of ears heard their instructions. God provides again.

We had such great support. God says He is the shield around us and the lifter of our heads. I watched this play out in practical ways. Our friends brought a yummy Indian meal then after we had our regular scheduled prayer meeting in our own family room. It was good to have Michael present even though he was very sleepy. Neighbors visited while others brought fresh-baked cookies. Another friend from my Bible study brought a meal and the love kept on coming. I am over-whelmed by the kindness of God!

I see God's gracious hand in so many details:

Michael did NOT suffer a heart attack.

He wasn't on the Great Wall of China in an emergency situation just one month earlier. Instead he was home in a controlled environment with doctors and technicians around him when he had his treadmill stress test.

Mike and Barb from church prayed for us the Sunday before we went in for the stress test. Their story was like a script of what really happened three days later to us. It was like we'd been through a medical dress rehearsal. God goes before us and prepares in advance the things we are to do.

We had such support, prayer and meals from friends and family.

We have a God who listens and is attentive to our cries.

We were able to spend Thanksgiving with our friends Jim and Linda, Susie and Ron, and Don and the many "kids" including our own. HAPPY THANKSGIVING!

So that's what I got for my birthday that year and I'd have to say it was a really great unplanned day. It still blows me away to read my journal entry/prayer to God from two days before "THAT DAY." You can go back to the beginning and reread it. Amazing!

This journal entry is from a few days after Michael's heart surgery:

The Lord says my daughter, my love…wait on Me. I work on your behalf. I am with you. You never have to be afraid. Never. Delight yourself in Me and I will give you the desires of your heart. Lay down your concern for Michael because I have already shown you that I preserve and keep him. I am the one who has been watching over him all his life. I watched over him in China, in the backyard, while he was at work, and during his treadmill-stress test. I will continue to go before him in all things. Relax Rachel, really, lower your shoulders and REST in my constant love. I will lead you, I will instruct you. I will teach you. I make a way for you. It is my purposes and plans that remain. I can do more in one move of My hand than you can in all your planning or fretting.

Usually a birthday gift is wrapped; it is something you want or need and it may even be a surprise. My birthday gift of 2011 was wrapped in God's love, timing, details, and provision and was tied with a big red bow: His people. Yes, my husband's good health is something I wanted and needed and the whole thing certainly was a surprise. For all of it I'm so grateful!

God used His people to remind me that He is always there.

Eighteen

Surprised by His Method

You've probably seen a movie where one character, a news anchor for instance, reads copy from a teleprompter and looks directly into the camera. She presses her finger to her ear and acknowledges the commands received from the hidden earpiece she's wearing while someone from a control room gives instructions to guide her. The scene goes something like this: "Stretch it a bit we're about to go to commercial" OR "Okay, welcome the mayor, we have him live, cued up from the onsite location and ready for his interview. Three, two, one, you're LIVE!"

I feel a bit like that. Although I do not wear a hidden earpiece, I receive commands and am asked questions. It's like the newsroom scene although it isn't audible. It's just a voice heard in my head. Other times, I've received the messages through visual signals first, then I hear His voice. It's the voice of the Master. He may teach, challenge, encourage, question, or warn. It may be just a simple voice of affirmation or His delight saying, "I love you!"

God speaks in subtle ways too. Many times He speaks while I walk. Perhaps it's being out in nature that makes me more aware of His presence. It could be the crisp air, the cool breeze, or even the trees that tower above and point my gaze upward to Him. I'm easily distracted and admittedly very flighty. So perhaps I'm less distracted outdoors, and more ready, fully tuned in and receptive. Creation testifies to the glory of God. He is the one who created all things. Maybe that's it! I'm not really sure. I do know I seem to hear Him when out walking. At first I listen to the rhythmic sound of my feet on the concrete, but as I continue to walk and think, my thoughts turn into conversations with Him. Like a radio station that needs to be dialed in, there may be static at first, but then as the dial is turned ever so slightly to the proper frequency, it becomes much clearer.

You guessed it I was out walking. I passed a blue two-story house with a lovely manicured yard. This lawn was deep green and beautifully edged along the sidewalk and the grass was recently mowed. I smelled it. My attention was drawn toward the sidewalk just a few feet to the left because I heard a strange sound originating from there. It sounded like heavy panting. Well, sort of and it left me puzzled and kind of freaked me out.

I looked more closely and saw two small sheltie dogs' snouts shoved right against the bottom of a white, wooden picket fence that lined this pristine property. The dogs breathed rapidly. The sound these two dogs made caused me to step back. I paused under the cool shade trees. The air felt damp. As I lingered there for a moment, I realized the dogs had lifted their snouts from under the fence and paced back and forth as they both attempted to bark at me, but couldn't. Neither one wore a collar, but they were unable to bark, even though each tried. The dogs only made a raspy, panting sound. They couldn't make a normal barking sound because their vocal chords were probably stripped. That's what caused them to make the wheezy-raspy sounds rather than a normal bark.

Okay, that's odd! As I continued on my normal trek, I clearly heard God whisper to me. *"Rachel, how will you use your voice? Will you speak up for Me? Will you testify about Me and sing My praises?"*

I wasn't sure why He asked me that. I'm still not sure. But His question caused me to think. *Was I reluctant to stand up for God? I wondered. Had I not been willing to speak up and testify about the goodness of God in my life and His presence in the hard times as well? Can my voice even be heard in my family, friendships and other areas of my influence? Do I speak up? OR am I more like a dog who lost her ability to bark?*

I do remember that I began to cry at His gentle question. I continued on and prayed, *"Lord, let me use my voice for You. Let me never be silenced or afraid to communicate truth. Let me share freely and openly. May I communicate both in a winsome manner and with the boldness of a lion if needed. Use my voice Lord and never let it be silenced, like stripped vocal cords, unable to even bark."*

Maybe He asks the same questions of you? Perhaps He is asking today as you read this. I'll repeat His question. Just replace my name with yours. "_____, how will you use your voice? Will you speak up for Me? Will you testify about Me and sing My praises?"

Psalm 63:3 Because your love is better that Life my lips will glorify you.

Nineteen

Turn Around and Go

Inside!

One autumn day, as I walked by a rather large terra-cotta colored house, I noticed some of the leaves that had collected on the sidewalk were the same color as the home. I shuffled my feet through the deep leaves which caused a wonderful swooshing sound. Next, I marched on them to hear them crunch instead. Then, above the noise of the leaves, I heard a ruckus. In the distance, stood a father yanking suitcases and Walmart bags from a hatchback as he loudly yelled and swore at his teenage daughter. She stood beside him throwing the same bags he had just removed back into her car. I was a bit embarrassed, concerned and uncomfortable. It was an awkward moment. So before I was directly upon them, I crossed over and I went to the other side of the street. He continued to use foul language as he pulled the sacks out of her car's hatchback again and threw them on the driveway. She thrust her body forward, pointed and hollered, "I hate you! Stop it! Stop it Dad! Those are MINE! I'm leaving!"

I felt like I'd been stung by a swarm of bees that I'd unintentionally disturbed. It seemed as though the bees had stung my head. Harsh words really affect me and those words kept coming back into my head over and over. I walked an additional few miles, but the words rung and stung again and again. It was just horrible. My spirit was troubled, but I resolved to pray for her daily. I thought it would be easy since her street was part of my normal route. I walked past her house almost every day. So I continued to pray as I passed, pray as I passed, pray as I passed for a long time. Then my walking partner changed and I no longer took that particular street.

Finally in early spring, before I headed out for my walk, I submitted my day to God and asked, *LORD this is Your day. Please order it and put me in the path of people of Your design and choosing.* I'll never forget what happened.

I wore my husband's fluorescent, highlighter yellow jacket. It's a polar-fleece lining from his winter coat, but it hung in the closet as I headed out on my walk so I grabbed it. I glanced in the mirror and chuckled because it was too big and made me look like a blinking neon sign, "NOTICE ME!" But I headed out anyway.

After many absent months, I found myself again on her street. And I saw her. I saw the same young, probably high school aged girl with long blond hair that stuck out beneath her yarn cap. She wore jeans and a light sweater. Even though it was spring, it was quite cold outside. I thought, *Burr ! You need a coat young lady.* She threw a pillow, some bags, and a backpack in the black hatchback and she yelled, "I mean it mom! I am leaving!"

The mother sat on the concrete porch front step of the house with a cordless phone in her hand waving it like a police officer waves a traffic baton as she pointed it toward the door of the house. She too was hollering, "No you're not. Get back in here. Get inside!" This volley of anger went back and forth for a while until the mother, who was also coatless, rose from the step, opened the front door and exclaimed, "I'm callin' the police!" She then disappeared.

By this time, I had walked past all the commotion and was headed up a slight hill, but looked back for a second to see what the girl would do. At that moment, my feet were literally arrested in their place and I couldn't move! So, with my neck craned back toward her, my feet planted as if cemented to the ground, I stood there frozen and looked at her as I began to pray. *Go back inside. Go back in. God, please help this sweet one go inside!* Now I know that her home environment was not good and I know that I probably didn't have the full story either. Having said that, I realize being on the street or a runaway's lifestyle is not a pleasant thing so that was what I prayed.

I stood statue-like and watched her. She plodded behind her car, looped around it near the path toward the house, and paused, but didn't go all the way in. Instead, she looked up the hill at me and screamed, "HEY! LADY ya got a blankin' starin' problem?" Then she climbed the few steps and went inside the front door. I remember asking God, "Okay! Am I good to go now?"

Saddened by the whole matter, I continued to walk home and prayed, *God, if I could ever get a chance to speak truth to that young lady I would, if you'd allow me.* I was expectant as I made my way up and down the hills around her neighborhood. Every car that passed I'd look to see whose it was, in case it was hers. As I left her immediate neighborhood, a car slowed a bit, but it was a young man. Rounding the bend, another car passed me, traveling more quickly. As it zoomed by, I realized that it was her! I recognized the car and driver. It was a young women whose cream colored knit cap was pulled down with her blonde hair sticking out beneath. She whizzed by me so quickly, but I knew it was her. I left the sidewalk immediately and ran into the middle of the street where the white lines are. On raised tippy toes, I waved my hands back and forth, like I was doing jumping jacks, as I tried to get her attention.

I remained in the middle of the street until I watched her travel past my house and down the bend. Then she disappeared from view. *"Oh, man! I wanted to talk to her, you know I would have, Lord. Have her come back, please! I want to talk to her!"* But she was gone.

A bit dejected, but somewhat relieved too I guess, I continued on. Suddenly, I saw the front of her little black car approach. Remember, I was wearing a fluorescent highlighter yellow polar fleece jacket. There was no mistaking me for me. She headed directly toward me and my stomach and heart seemed to switch places. I prayed, *"Okay, okay, God what am I gonna say? What should I say Lord?"* In my spirit, I heard him say, *"I'll give you words!"* So, I left the sidewalk again and went back into the middle of the street and watched as she began to slowly roll down her driver's window as she drew near.

I spoke first, "You know what? I might not have a staring problem, but I might have a caring problem! Are you all right?"

"Yeah, I'm sorry about that!" she said.

"It's okay. I'm Rachel."

"Hello, I'm Suzie" she replied.

I continued, "I don't know what you think about this, but I believe that God wants me to talk to you. You see, I have been by your home a few times and I have heard the words spoken over you and I know that you're very wounded. I'm so sorry Suzie."

She commented, "Yeah, it's not much longer and then I'll graduate and get out of there!"

"I'm not sure what you think about this at all, but could I pray for you?" I asked.

VOOM! At what seemed to be the speed of light, I watched her as she bowed her head, squeezed her eyes tightly and folded her hands in one fluid motion. So I stuck my head inside her car. I don't really remember my prayer exactly. But God does. I think I prayed that she would come to understand that there is a God who loves her. I prayed, *God I know You made Suzie and You have a plan for her life. I know that You have a future for her and a hope if she comes to know You. I prayed that she would know that, like the Psalmist prayed, even though my father and mother forsake me the Lord will not reject me.* I prayed for her safety. And maybe some other stuff too. I can get going when I talk with God. When I finished I said, *In Jesus name, Amen!* She raised her little head and used the back side of her shirt sleeve to wipe her nose and her tears.

I asked Suzie where she was going and she said she was going over to stay at a girlfriend's house in a neighboring suburb. I said, "Do you see that light gray house? That is where I live Suzie and if you ever need anything, come to my door.

"No, I'm fine," she said and she pulled away. I have prayed for Suzie off and on for years. I stopped typing to pray for her a moment ago. I prayed from part of Psalm 40:

I waited patiently for the LORD; He turned to me and He heard my cry.

He lifted me out of the slimy pit, out of the mud and mire; He set my feet on a rock and gave me a firm place to stand. He put a new song in my mouth a hymn of praise to our God. Many will see in fear and put their trust in the LORD.

You can pray for her too. I find it so interesting and great of the Lord Jesus to remind me as I'm writing this book that the prayer I prayed near the fence of the bark-less dogs which was, "Lord, please help me not be voiceless, but always use my voice to tell of You," He honored later. Lord because Your love is better than life, my lips will glorify You. Thank you for an opportunity to use my voice to talk to and pray for Suzie.

Twenty

The "Norm!" Thing

Do you know the theme song to Cheers? How it talks about going to a place where everybody knows your name? Well, when I lived in the Minneapolis area, I felt like I knew everyone. I was so accustomed to being known while living in the Minneapolis area. I refer to it as my "NORM!" years. On Cheers, the heavy, curly-haired character Norm would enter the bar the same way every time. The response to his arrival was the same every time too. Upon his entrance, all the people in the bar would simultaneously announce his arrival, hollering, "NORM!" Their simple greeting said a great deal. Norm! It meant "How's it going?," "Glad you're here!," "What's up?" and "Come on in. Join us!" All in one exclamation. "NORM!"

I was used to that type of recognition and familiarity in Minnesota. People knew me and I knew them. I was accustomed to the "NORM" thing. Whether I entered my church, attended a mom's meeting, gathered with others at a homeschool co-op campus, walked down the sidewalk in my neighborhood or even headed to my mailbox, I heard it, the welcomed call, "RACHEL!" I was relationally rich!

Then we moved to Wisconsin.   I had to start all over again, at a "Ground Zero" of sorts. I truly like people, but this felt exhausting, exciting, difficult and wonderful all at the same time. I had to do the work of meeting people, introducing myself and my children. I had to explain everything because there was NO history, no back story with anyone. No "NORM!" experience at all. It was really hard and I was lonely.

Except for one couple that we've known our entire married life, we knew no one. So I had to start my collection of friends from scratch. I felt alone. I just wanted to cry. I missed knowing and being known. Can you hear the music in your head? *"Where everybody knows your name, and they're always glad you came. You wanna be where you can see, our troubles are all the same. You wanna be where everybody knows Your name."* Okay, okay gradually fade the music. Still quieter, please.

Yup! Ground Zero was difficult for me and taxing! Building something takes time. I remember what part of my neighborhood I was walking in when I prayed, *God, you know that I need to be in community and I need friends.* (By the way these needs of mine are universal. You need this too.) This longing is of God.

I heard God, *I'm the friend that sticks closer than a brother.* He reassured me that with Him there wasn't relational drama or competitiveness, or difficulty in schedules to meet together. He also impressed upon me that I was to draw close to Him and he would give me the desire of my heart - Himself! He knew that more of Him was what I really needed. It still is. He answered that prayer AND He gave me friends too.

God, the King of the universe, was impressing on me that HE WAS my friend. Just the thought of that blows my mind. He is the one I was really looking for and in my spirit I knew He had plans to also bring girlfriends into my life. God delivered on His plans. I am richer, I believe, for persevering. Because of moving, I have collected some really great friends! I can't think of my life without my entire collection. God has used each of my friends from all the states I've lived in to help make me who I am today. Girlfriends as well as couples too.

These friends are the ones who have cheered for me, prayed for me and even challenged me. So to those friends of mine, who have prayed for me, loved me, challenged me to continue with my "communication" now venturing into writing, you know who you are, and I say thank you for making me feel the "NORM!" thing again. Even now I'm feeling it so strongly. I love you TONS! I could just squeeze you all!

A friend loves at all times, and a brother is born for a time of adversity. Proverbs 17:17 In friendship, I am very rich. I've been blessed by God.

Every good and perfect gift is from above, coming down from the Father of heavenly lights, who does not change like shifting shadows. James 1:17

My Prayer: *Lord, thank you for being my friend. You have blessed my life through rich friendships. I pray a blessing on the friends in my life, right now in the name of Jesus. Thank you for the things that You have taught me through each one of my friends. I ask that if the reader who is holding this book right now is lonely, that You, Lord Jesus, would be their friend. Please bring other people into their life now for mutual encouragement. I pray for these friends to spur one another on to love and good deeds. Thank you that You orchestrate things. Thank you that You have a good plan for all of our lives and that You are able to do this. In Jesus name, Amen.*

Twenty-one

Bird Splat

I blew into the steaming, caramel colored liquid then tentatively sipped my hot coffee cupped in both hands while seated upstairs in my family room loft. I read these verses:

Psalm 119:105 Your word is a lamp to my feet and a light for my path.

Psalm 119:112 My heart is set on keeping your decrees to the very end.

I reflected on God's word being the light for our paths. I prayed, *God please be my guide and Michael's too. As we chart our paths clearly guide us, redirect u*s or even stop us if needed.

I was STILL and so was the room. Morning time is like that in this house. The quietness was my companion. Suddenly, BOOM! It sounded like a canon had been shot off. I mean, it was seriously loud! It startled me big time! I flinched at the sound and nearly spilled my coffee. What in the WORLD?

A bird hit the window nearest me. BOOM!! No Joke. I felt badly about the crazy bird. *Am I going to need to go around the house to see if he died?* I wondered. *Gross! Wait, perhaps he was just stunned for a moment and flew away.*

As I glanced up, there was still evidence on the window of the bird's beak striking and then a squiggly mark trailing down the window's glass as though a child had used a white crayon to make a wax doodle. "That mark's from its beak!" I said aloud amazed, even though I was alone. "And there's wing evidence too!" A cloudy outline of the "SPLAT" complete with tiny cream colored feathers blew in the wind, still attached to the outside window.

I'd been praying that God would clearly guide us. That is why the lamp to my feet verse Psalm 119:105 resonated. "Lord don't let us go in the wrong direction. Stop us if we are not to go down certain paths. God be the lamp for my feet and a light for my path."

You, reader are probably thinking, why don't you put something in your windows so that birds don't keep hitting the windows? You know they make stickers for that, right? Those poor crazy birds someone help them! WAIT! That is not my point!

The point is my prayer to God was please stop us in our tracks so we don't ever disappoint You or head in the wrong direction. I uttered that prayer right when the bird splat happened. I guess God was telling me He'd stop me dead in my tracks if He needed to. I hope to be very obedient and not need to be stunned or killed like the poor birds were.

Again, spiritual truths were being taught to me in tangible and visual ways. Just like the lily pads I saw one summer as God spoke truth to me. He still speaks all the time. Am I listening? Are you?

Twenty-two

Roadblocks to Food

"**D**o you want to go with me to the store and run a few errands?" I asked Grace. I assured her it wouldn't take too long. She would be off to college in the fall so I desperately wanted to spend as much time with her as possible. Running errands and being in the car together listening to music was always fun for us. She said, "Sure!"

I heard Grace grab the car key from our key box as she shouted, "I'll be in the car!"

When I got to the car, she was on her cell phone placing an order, "Yes, I'd like one order of Japanese pan noodles with chicken for pick up please." That's odd we just ate lunch together. As we reached the end of our street, Grace began to pull out to make a left but was nearly t-boned by a woman in a white mini-van. "Whoa! Whoa! Whoa!" she cried. We were both a bit dazed. "That was close!" we exclaimed in unison.

Grace stopped at her bank to deposit a few checks. It was a beautiful summer day. So I jumped out of the car. I looked at the flowers set out in a temporary garden center outside the corner grocery store adjacent to her bank. I was mesmerized by color and beauty. I hoped to buy some annuals but realized that I didn't have my debit card with me. *Oh brother, I won't be able to pay for any flowers or my groceries.* When we both returned to the car, I told Grace. She said, "Mom, you can just use mine and pay me back later."

So we set off for Noodles & Co. to pick up her order. She grabbed it, hurried back to the car and off we went again to Pick and Save for a few items that Aldi doesn't carry. Grace stayed in the car to eat her Japanese Pan noodles while they were hot.

Finally, we headed toward Aldi but she missed the street. "No big deal," I said. We cut through the parking lots of a few local businesses. Our route lead us through downtown Waukesha near Carroll University and then to the Aldi. As we traveled, we encountered many "road closed ahead" signs and barricades at multiple intersections. Wow! We backtracked, retraced our steps, traveled roads we'd never been on, and then we almost hit a young woman pedestrian. She was wearing headphones, jaywalking, and was oblivious to all cars, including ours.

As we encountered more "road closed ahead" signs, Grace accepted the challenge and maneuvered through the open roads like a kid in a corn maze. Red light. We stopped. That's when a semi driver almost hit us because he couldn't maneuver his truck around the corner tightly enough. I turned toward Grace wide-eyed and asked, "How many close calls is that?" Immediately, the car directly in front of us slowed unexpectedly and Grace reacted quickly. *What now? Why is THIS guy stopping?* He had stopped suddenly so that a frizzy-auburn haired woman, wearing a black boot cast on her right foot could hobble across the road. I am not making this stuff up! We chuckled because it seemed like something from a Saturday Night Live skit or scene from a wacky comedy. "Seriously? We're just trying to go get some groceries!"

At the next stop sign Grace said, "Mom that's how it is when we are just trying to get some spiritual food–the Word of God. We are distracted, roadblocks appear everywhere, road closed ahead signs even simple distractions can keep us from our daily bread."

Grace, who had lived with me her entire life, got it! She too saw spiritual truth in ordinary and everyday situations. That balmy summer day, she helped me make a connection between the tangible everyday situations and spiritual truth.

After about another mile, we pulled into Aldi and parked. Grace requested I remain in the car while she finished eating. So I did. Not one to sit idle, I gathered my grocery bags, got my quarter for the cart, located my list in my cavernous purse and even pulled from it my trusty sharpie marker.

Then I sat. I watched people leave the store with carts full of junk food. I told Grace I would love to stop people and say, "Wait one second! Please just look in your cart. This isn't food, take this back, this back and this back. None of that food has any nutritional value! You can keep only these few items."

Grace said, "Mom that would be so rude! " I told her how sad I get when people foolishly think that food, devoid of any nutrients, is going to fill them with what their body truly needs. Once again, I connected food with our spiritual walk. We often fill the carts of our lives with things that we think will satisfy but in reality it's just junk. Whether it's television, home improvement projects, new cars or jobs, we fill up our spiritual carts hoping to find satisfaction. But only God satisfies.

By the way, what God was teaching me did not stop there. Once He gets me tuned in, opening my eyes and heart to His spirit, He continues. We shopped and as we headed to the checkout lane, Grace mentioned, "Mom, I can't believe how many things I avoided throwing into the cart today because I am not hungry. I had such a satisfying lunch of noodles that I'm not grabbing all the other items I see."

Yes, I've given her the advice, Don't go to the grocery store hungry, you'll spend more money and buy things your body doesn't really need. Again, in my spirit I heard God say, *Rachel, when you are full of Me and satisfied in Me, you will not even desire the things that don't satisfy, that promise to fulfill but will only leave you empty.*

Let me ask you. Are you letting roadblocks stop you from getting to Jesus, the bread of life? Are you filled with "junk food" and are no longer hungry for what truly satisfies?

Then Jesus declared, *"I am the bread of life. Whoever comes to me will never go hungry, And whoever believes in me will never be thirsty."* John 6:35 NIV

Well, we finally got the groceries we came to get! Phew! I had promised Grace it wouldn't take too long. Oops! But we were determined. Even with close calls, near accidents, road closed signs and multiple distractions, we still made to it Aldi. Nothing stopped us from gathering the food we needed

P.S. Now that we knew the way, you'll be pleased to know our ride home was rapid, unobstructed, safe and a whole lot of fun.

Twenty-three

Escorted With Care

Events for college students start around my bedtime. Perhaps it's when the students are most alert, but frankly, I'm nearly exhausted. I was asked to speak to a group called The AVE, comprised of college students, in downtown Milwaukee late at night. I was to "fill in" for Laurie who got the stomach flu. She called and said, "Rachel, you are the only person I'm calling and if you are unable, I'll try to gut it out tonight."

The cool "God part" was just a few days earlier I was reading the book, <u>Married for Life</u> by Stuart and Jill Briscoe as I walked on the treadmill. In one chapter, Jill mentioned speaking to college students. In my heart I thought, *I'd really like to do that, speak to college students!* I never shared it with my prayer partner, wrote it down in my journal or voiced it to anyone. It was simply an unspoken desire of my heart.* This call from Laurie who had been vomiting, came just a few days later. With just five hour's notice, I agreed to do it.

I hung up the phone. Immediately, questions ran through my mind and a few fears too: *I also lead Bible study tonight, will I make it in time? I have no time to prepare. Wow! That's quite late to begin the meeting, isn't it? Where will I park? I don't know for sure how to get there. I'll have to look it up on MapQuest and print it out.*

I can hear you laughing, but this was what one did back then. It was before smart phones and GPS. I was still quite tentative, but paused briefly to pray.

God reminded me of his promise to bless my coming and going both now and forever. He said, *"Rachel you want to do this and I can't bless your coming and going if you never come or go. Now go!"*

I left church in a scurry, after leading Bible study, a bit tired and very thirsty. I exited the building, made no eye contact in the halls so I wouldn't "get stuck" in conversation with anyone. I didn't have time to stop, use the bathroom or get a much needed drink of water. No time! I wanted to make it. On time. I made it to the car in the frigid temperatures and questioned going downtown by "myself" at night, even though Marquette and UW Milwaukee's campuses are both right there.

I drove, one hand holding the chilly steering wheel, the other my set of printed directions. The dome light was on, then off. On, then off. On, then off so I could read my printed paper. It was quite a way downtown in the winter air and in dark of night. I'm so thirsty! *Almost there! Around the corner. Okay, there's the mentioned "RED DOOR" of the building.*

I found a parking spot, the ONLY space left in the tiny lot RIGHT beside the building. Delighted I cried, "Thank you, Lord Jesus!" I ascended the steps, reached for the door's handle, but didn't pull it because it opened for me instead. A friendly greeter locked eyes with mine and warmly said, "Welcomed to 'the Ave' you must be Rachel?" She extended her hand and I wondered if she wanted me to shake it, but she handed me, get this...a water bottle! I was so grateful. "Thank you, I am so thirsty!" I told her.

Next, I was ushered through the large auditorium with its high ceilings, I heard my heels as they struck the wooden flooring and echoed through the room. I was escorted down a winding narrow staircase to the basement, where a small team prayed over me and the evening's event. All of my preconceived worries and concerns were gone! *God, you bless my coming and going both now and forever more. Thanks!*

Psalm 121:7,8 The LORD will keep you from all harm—he will watch over your life; the LORD will watch over your coming and going both now and forever more. NIV

*Delight yourself in the Lord, and he will give you the desires of your heart. Psalm 37:4 ESV

I saw Jill Briscoe a few weeks later, a sweet mentor, who speaks all over the world, literally, all over the world. We chatted, I told her EVERY detail, EVERY concern of mine was so specifically answered, sovereignly met. She said,"Oh yes! Rachel, that's your 'traveling angel' doing so well, taking care of you so that you feel the comfort of the Lord and His protection over your speaking ministry." I'm certain God allowed those tiny details to be taken care of in the beginning so that I would trust Him with greater details as I went along. I believe I have. As you read this, understand that He knows the desires of your heart and He blesses your coming and going too.

Twenty-four

Big Driving Day!

Daily I ask God to bless my speech and my heart from which words flow. I am amazed at the truth of this proverb.

A gentle answer turns away wrath, but a harsh word stirs up anger. Proverbs 15:1

The importance of using a gentle answer was made clear to me when my son Michael first learned to drive. Michael went to the DMV to get his driver's permit. Like a typical fifteen and a half year old, he was eager to drive. He and my husband left the house together, excitedly. "Let's go get your permit!" I heard my husband shout as they exited. Then, when, they returned I heard my proud spouse exclaim, "Honey, he PASSED!"

"Yay! Let me see it!" I said excited for Michael.

"Well, you'll have to go back in with him on Monday to get the actual permit," my husband informed me.

"What?" I retorted.

They were disappointedly sent away because my son Michael wasn't officially 15 1/2 years old yet. (It was September 30 and his birthday is March 31. We reasoned that might be the half year point. Because there are only thirty days in September, not thirty one, and it was Friday, they went in to the DMV. It made complete sense to all of us.) Anyway, they were told they needed to come back to obtain his permit the following Monday, October 4.

My husband desired to go back but had to work. So, I'm the one that had to take him back in on Monday. So I did. I thought, *this is going to be a breeze! Michael has already taken AND passed his test. All we have to do is pay and get our hands on his "permit" and then he can even DRIVE home. He'll be thrilled to do that!*

We pulled into the parking lot on the crisp fall day super pumped up! The emotions quickly changed, because the line was so long it extended all the way out the entrance into the parking lot. "Oh NO!" *I'm sure everyone thought going a bit before the lunch hour to beat the rush was a great idea.* "Oh, okay let's go!"

I didn't WANT to stand in line, we were pressed for time and needed to get back to school. A thought struck me: *If you don't want to stand in line, Rachel, it could be a pride issue. Do you somehow think your time is more precious than other peoples?* So, I decided to be patient. But Michael had already stood in the line the other day so I decided to inquire about how to best continue and find out if we had to stand in line at all.

I left my son standing in line for a moment, walked to the side of the room, and asked a little blonde woman holding a clipboard, "Excuse me, my son has already taken and passed his permit test on Friday, but then he was told he had to come back today. Could you tell me, are we in the proper line?"

"No, this line is for a different process. You can stand right under that 'test correction' sign. Do you see it?" she asked as she extended her arm and pointed in the direction of the sign hanging above. She continued, "When they call your number, give them your name, they will see that his name is already in the system, marked passed."

We expressed our gratitude and watched as she escorted a young man into one of the rooms and closed the door behind her. Probably a terrified young individual about to take his "behind the wheel" exam we surmised.

So Michael and I smiled at a few people, "excuse us, pardon me, thank you" as we wove our way directly under the test correction sign. I sat in the waiting area and let Michael handle the details. It's all part of growing up, right? I took a seat in the waiting area and I was poised nonchalantly looking through a few magazines while I waited.

Suddenly, a woman hollered, "NEXT!"

Michael stepped forward and excitedly explained, "Hi, I was here on Friday, passed my permit test and now I just need to pay for it. Here is my passport."

Michael has always been very polite and I was proud of him as I watched from where I was seated. I glanced up from time to time because I was the one that held the checkbook that he would soon need.

I noticed Michael look at me with distressed and urgent eyes, *come over here NOW mom!* I could hear the woman behind the counter begin to question him.

"Which line did you stand in? You didn't even stand in a line. You cannot just bring your passport. On PAGE 2 of the handbook it clearly states that you have to have your Social Security card! Son, do you HAVE your social security card?"

Michael explained that his driving instructor had told his whole class that they needed a form of ID. It could be a passport or your Social Security card but to bring it in at the time you take the test to obtain your permit.

She continued to press him. "Well, on PAGE 2 of the handbook it clearly states that you need to have your Social Security card."

A bit confused, Michael immediately snapped his head toward the waiting area looking at me like, *Seriously, Mom get over here!* BUT I was already walking over.

I approached the counter and asked, "Is there a problem?" The woman behind the counter said,"He has his passport, but on PAGE 2 of the handbook, it CLEARLY states that you are to have your Social Security card! By the way what line did you stand in?" I remember thinking WOW! *This woman is really adamant about PAGE 2 of the handbook! Seriously?* I then remembered pleasant words...a gentle answer. Remember, Rachel. A gentle answer turns away wrath. I began to pray, silently in my own heart and mind. I am not kidding, in my flesh I would not have had a gentle answer because this lady was just laying into my son. So, the "mama bear protecting her cub thing" was really raging strongly on the inside of me. *Don't mess with him or you'll mess with me!* But through the power of the Holy Spirit, I was able to respond. *Lord, this woman probably deals with angry, frustrated, impatient people all day and she is angry and she is frustrated and she is impatient. PLEASE, please, Lord, help me speak pleasant words to her.*

So with my voice pitched up a bit higher than usual, I began to answer, "When we first walked in, we asked a lady who had long blonde hair and was holding a clipboard where we should stand and she directed us to stand under the 'test correction' sign. I don't see her now because she went into that room over there and closed the door."

She responded again with her mantra: "Well, you have to stand in a line!" Blah blah blah. "On PAGE 2 of the handbook it clearly states that you MUST have your Social Security card!" Blah blah blah blah.

Don't be so STUCK on this PAGE 2 of the handbook! I pitched my voice up higher and higher about to sound like Alvin the chipmunk as I breathed a prayer, *Holy Spirit flow through me.*

Then I replied, "Okay! If we need his social security card, that's not a problem. How 'bout we just get in the car, drive back home to get it, and return. When we get back here, Ma'am, what line should we stand in?"

I really wasn't trying to be snippy. I was thinking a gentle answer turns away wrath.

She realized that she was just being ugly to us. Suddenly, CRAZILY! MIRACULOUSLY! She was completely transformed. She hung her head slightly, shaking it a bit as she said hushed and sheepishly, "Well, you really don't have to do that!"

Lickety-split. She signed all the papers, rapidly stamped all the documents loudly. Bam bam bam. I wrote out the check for the permit, pressed it against the perforation, ripped it from the checkbook, and smiled as we thanked her for her time and wished her a good day.

"Son, you can drive if you want!" I said as I tossed him the keys.

A harsh word stirs up anger, but a gentle answer turns away wrath. It can be done. I'm here to testify. The Holy Spirit is always present and ready to be employed with HIS power! Man, pleasant words were a bonus on the DMV permit day. Scripture says *the right word at the right time is like a custom-made piece of jewelry.* I do love the right word at the right time and I love a good piece of jewelry! And Michael, well he loves cars and driving to this day!

Twenty-five

Could it be an Idol?

God hates it when we pursue, serve, or are emotionally drawn to other gods which are not really gods at all. I don't think we really believe we have idols in our lives. But we do. An idol may be a thing or person, that we form our identity around. From where does our identity come? Like many young males my son Michael can easily places his identity in his wheels. For him it was his motorcycle.

Psalm 106:36 They worshiped their idols, which became a snare to them.

Isaiah 45:16 All the makers of idols will be put to shame and disgraced; they will go off into disgrace together.

This is a prayer I prayed for myself and each of my family members: *No idols, Lord. Only You, the one true God! Let us all love and serve only You.* It's a blanket prayer, broadly covering anything that could compete for our love, attention, worship of Him. *Lord, cast down any idols that are in your rightful place.*

My daughter Grace, our friend Alex, and I headed to the university to pick up Michael Heggen and bring him home for the summer. We were excited to be reunited. We moved some things directly over into his apartment for the next fall semester, but gathered the rest of his belongings into our van for the trip home. The whole duel moving process was lengthy and tiring. Just the thought of our four hour drive home made us eager to get moving before dark.

Grace, Alex and I piled into the van, along with what seemed like one million items! Michael rode his motorcycle and we followed behind. He requested, "Mom will you lead because I had a funny problem earlier in the day with my motorcycle and I had to charge the battery before heading out and I just pulled it off the charger."

I agreed. "Sure, no problem!"

We hadn't gone more than 15 – 20 miles when I saw him, in my rearview mirror, pull off onto the shoulder of the interstate. So I quickly pulled the van over too. Michael said, "The bike is really acting up!" We attempted again, this time he was in the front leading us, but very quickly he pulled off the road. So I did too. He slowed to a stop, removed his helmet and walked to the van where we were parked.

He said, "I can't ride it at all. It feels like someone's pulling on the chain making it start and stop, it's lurching like a bucking bronco." We'd passed a road sign, so we knew we were somewhere close to Eau Claire. *Wow! That's still four hours from home! That's another day that we'll have to come back if we abandon the bike now! Consider too the gas money, time and inconvenience!* All the factors needing to be thought through and the questions bounced in my brain like ping pong balls being tossed back and forth. *Should we leave it? Should we try to haul it or rent a trailer for it?*

We prayed for wisdom and supernatural favor. As we discussed: Where to leave it? Should we leave it? Should we try to transport it on a trailer? Troubleshooting as a group, we wondered, *do we dare put the motorcycle inside the van? If we do give it a try, will it fit?*

"I'm not sure if we could lift it because the side of the road is so slanted and steep." I said. *The first step up into the van was quite high. We'd have to consider that if we chanced it.* We decided to try and planned to execute a "Tetris" move of Michael's stuff to accommodate his heavy motorcycle. *"Okay, let's move these boxes and put the wheels out at an angle, that might work!"* Michael said. We were still considering the options when a police officer pulled behind us and sat in his car a while. Perhaps he was running our license plates or something I'm not sure, but after awhile he exited his car and asked, "What's going on?"

"Broken down motorcycle!" Michael explained. We saw God's supernatural favor flow, the officer was very kind and helpful. He went back to his car, filled out a report that said we could leave it on the side of the road without being ticketed.

When the officer returned he casually asked, "How much does this motorcycle weigh?"

"400 pounds," Michael answered. Then I witnessed their nonverbal communication: heads nodding and shoulders shrugging and a final, head nodding toward the van. I got the message! They'd communicated in a split second, *Well, let's do it, it's worth a try for sure. Why not? Alright, here we go!*

Alex held one handlebar, Michael and the police officer lifted the bike seat and Grace guided it from the front. My role was to remain seated, in the driver's seat, neck cranked around like an owl, as far to the right as possible to smile at them, encourage them, and pray. *Please God, please!*

Michael desperately hoped to close the door. With head cocked, he gave one of those, unsure and suspenseful glances that sent the message, *everyone hold your breath and we'll see,* BAM! The van door shut! "YESSSSS! IT FITS!" Michael exclaimed, we screamed and the cheers rang out.

As we traveled together down the road, Michael was clearly upset about owning a non-working motorcycle. He was very quiet. He sat pinned behind the passenger's seat and his metal beast. Cramped on the van floor beside his prized possession and object of utter frustration, he sat dejected. Although deflated, he handled the disappointment well.

I was sad to see him upset. "Oh, son, I am so sorry." I admitted that I had been praying against any idols in our lives. I told Michael I wasn't praying FOR THIS to happen, but confessed my prayer that all idols in our lives to be cast down. That we'd all be honest about any thing that we grip so tightly we won't let go because all idols WILL topple. "It's sure hard to hold this motorcycle as an idol when our tired, 15 year old van has to transport it home, right? Of course I want your motorcycle fixed son. I do hope that you get this problem figured out and running again because it is your transportation this summer. But it is quite apparent that it is not the case for tomorrow and that it has, at least for a time, toppled down from a lofty place of honor." I said.

It had toppled once, and although now fixed, I hope in his heart it will remain just a piece of metal. Ironically God continued to answer my prayer and began to topple idols in my life shortly after this motorcycle episode. One by one things I may have held too tightly have been dismantled and taken from me. Do you remember my prayer? This is it: *Lord, cast down anything, anyone, any idols that are in Your rightful place.*

Twenty-six

In Step with the Spirit

My husband and I were headed out on a walk the other day and we both set our phones for an exercise app that logs mileage and heart rate and our path's distance. We typically push the start button at the same time, "Ready? Start!" that way the mileage marked remains in sync. Our legs are roughly the same length, but our stride was off. So I did a little hop step-ball-change to get my stride equal with his. For the first part of our trek, I was holding his hand. It wasn't until I did that step-ball-change to get our stride in sync that it became easy. Before that, I was bopping around and tugging against his hand rather than our arms swinging like a pendulum, the motion feeling fluid.

I know how it is to keep in step with the Spirit. There are times when I need to, through prayer, adjust my step to keep it more in line with what God is doing. Lately, I've really been praying to stay in step with the Spirit, not to run ahead, even with this book. But certainly not to lag behind in the leading of the Holy Spirit. My prayer is as Michael and I transition into this empty nest phase, keeping in step with the Spirit the whole time, we will continue to have the spiritual vision that we need to recognize the ways in which God is leading. *Galatians 5:25 Since we live by the Spirit, let us keep in step with the Spirit.*

My prayer also is that I would rest in the knowledge that God is a promise keeping God and I can trust His promises. I want to be like Abraham who didn't waver in unbelief. This section from Romans 4:17-24 *As it is written: "I have made you a father of many nations." He is our father in the sight of God, in whom he believed – the God who gives life to the dead and calls things that are not as though they were. Against all hope, Abraham in hope believed and so he became the father of many nations, just as it had been said to him, "So show your offspring be." Without weakening in his faith, he faced the fact that his body was as good as dead–since he was about 100 years old–and that Sarah's womb was also dead. Yet he did not waiver through unbelief regarding the promise of God, but was strengthened in his faith and gave glory to God, being fully persuaded that God had power to do what he had promised this is why "it was credited to him as righteousness." The words "it was credited to him" were written not for him alone, but also for us, to whom God will credit righteousness – for us who believe in him who raised Jesus our Lord from the dead.*

The Holy Spirit is our teacher, comforter, and guide. The Holy Spirit dwells inside us as believers. The Holy Spirit doesn't just come and go. As a believer we are marked with the seal of the promised Holy Spirit. I want to keep in step with Him.

My prayer, I hope it is your prayer too, is to stay in step with the Spirit. There is no computer or phone app for that. It is a matter of the will and my obedience. To hear the still small voice of the Holy Spirit as He prompts, nudges or leads. I don't want to tug against His leading. I want to change my steps if needed. Just the way I did while walking with my honey. And I want to believe God like Abraham, *He is our father in the sight of God, in whom he believed –*

the God who gives life to the dead and calls things that are not as though they were. Abraham did believe even when it didn't make sense. He didn't waver. I don't want to waver in unbelief. Even though I have difficult things in my life right now. Nothing is too hard for God. Only God gives life to the dead. So I pray, *Lord help me keep in step with You help me not waver but believe.*

Twenty-seven

Call Me a Color Weirdo

Call me a color weirdo! As a daughter of an artist, I have been raised to view color in a certain way and observe it in everyday circumstances. I love to work with, design with and paint with color. As a young girl my dad would talk to me all the time about visual things. I loved spending time with him.

Often, as we were driving in the car, he'd ask, "Hey, Rachel, do you see that Chevrolet in the right lane? The green one? Do you see that front driver's door is a different color than its front panel bumper area? I'm sure that car has been in an accident." He'd continue to instruct me. "Notice the front panel, it has a little more yellow tint to the green color. It's lighter or a warmer green, right? Now look and compare that front panel to the door and the entire car. It's a bit bluer in its hue. Do you see it? I bet the front was smashed and replaced."

I learned so much from my dad this way. (Now that was when a great deal of work and color matching was done in the auto body shops rather than reordering parts from a car manufacturer.)

I've taken many of my father's painting and watercolor classes. Each year we mixed colors all day long the entire first day. Color after color was mixed, adding a little more warm or a little more cool to each paint combination to make neutrals. We had to mark down the   paint color selections ___+ ___ = ____ beside the swatch of color we just laid down on the paper. Then we knew what we had mixed to get the colors and their variations. We also learned to mix specific colors to make our "visual black." As a result, I can see very slight differences in color. Man, my father is a master at colors and I believe my eyes have been trained to see this way too.

Often friends ask my advice about color. Whether it's the color of tile or carpeting, paint for the walls or cedar colors for their decks, when they are remodeling or repainting they ask my opinion. My father taught me this phrase, "A meter of green is greener than a centimeter of green!" What that means is a larger amount of one color seems to be more of that color than just a little of it. That's important to remember when gazing at the endless selection of 2" x 2" square paint chips in the hardware store, local Menards or even Home Depot.

I received an emergency call once from a distressed friend who said, "HELP! I tried to select a pink for my walls, but it looks like I vomited Pepto-Bismol over my entire living room. Can you come over and help me?"

I heard my Dad then, "Remember Rachel, a meter of green is greener than a centimeter of green!" The more of that paint you put on the wall the more of that color it will become.

It applies to more than just paint. Let's say new homeowners need to replace the carpeting; medium brown is the final winner but when the carpet is laid in the whole room they hate it. They think it looks like an Iowa farm field's dark, black topsoil. That's because a meter of brown is browner than a centimeter of brown.

It's not like I have x-ray eyes or anything, but I do have a pretty good sense of color. I am thankful that I have been trained along the way to see these small visual color nuances. I got to thinking about how many people do not even see these small differences, when my daughter Grace was getting a tooth implant. We were looking at the color of her new tooth and I was talking with the dentist about it. I used some terms that made him snap his head to the right quickly and say, "Oh, I like that! You know what you're talking about."

I told him that I'm the daughter of an artist.

As Grace and I were driving to the next appointment to see the orthodontist, I was telling her a little bit about how my dad taught me these little things, at natural points, all the time and I, like a sponge, soaked them in. I have observed color and studied it with him often. He imparted this to me. Now it's part of the fabric of who I am and how I see, I guess. My son Michael has this keen color awareness/ability too and it is a joy to see him use it.

I was thinking about how our father God wants to train us in the everyday small things all along life's path; to "see" in the spiritual and eternal realms not just this natural and temporal one; and to learn His truth, fix them in our hearts and minds and pass them on to our children.

Deuteronomy 11:18,19 Fix these words of mine in your hearts and minds; tie them as symbols on your hands and bind them on your forehead. Teach them to your children, talking about them when you sit at home and when you walk along the road, when you lie down and when you get up.

I believe God is doing that all day in my life. In each situation, through every circumstance, in every meeting and during every encounter with people, he is with me and I'm learning. He wants me and you to stay spiritually fixed on Him and tuned in to the visual spiritual world and have our hearing tuned to His words of truth. I'm still learning from my heavenly Father and as I spend my time with Him He teaches me. He still speaks!

Your word is a lamp to my feet and a light for my path. Psalm 119:105

I will praise the LORD, who counsels me; even at night my heart instructs me. Psalm 16:7

John 10: 27 My sheep listen to my voice; I know them, and they follow me.

Apostle Paul prayed this for our eyes: *I pray also that the eyes of your heart may be enlightened in order that you may know the hope to which he has called you, the riches of his glorious inheritance in the saints, and his incomparably great power for us who believe. That power is like the working of his mighty strength, which he exerted in Christ when he raised him from the dead and seated him at his right hand in the heavenly realms. Ephesians 1:18-20*

My prayer: *Lord, make my spiritual eyesight keen. Allow me to see in the spiritual realm more clearly than I see in the natural one. God I ask that my ears would be in tune with Your voice and that I would hear it more loudly than any natural sound around me. Make me a "spiritual color" weirdo. In Jesus name, amen.*

Twenty-eight

Want to be Close to You

Do you know who David Phelps is? I really like him. He's a fabulous tenor who has sung for years with the Gaither Vocal Band and has had his own solo career as well. I've been known to repeatedly watch Gaither videos while folding laundry. When David Phelps flawlessly hits his famous high notes, I can barely stand it. I'm awestruck! I run downstairs to our piano (I don't even play the piano) but I try to find the note that he just sang because I'm amazed at his incredible vocal range. David Phelps singing "Oh Holy Night," "It is Well With My Soul," and even "Bring Him Home" from Les Mis all bring me to tears. I listen to his CDs, watch videos that he's in, attend his concerts and tell other people how wonderfully he sings. So my husband got us concert tickets for Mother's Day. Great gift idea! The concert was in early June and I was so excited to go.

The afternoon of the concert, I was cleaning and talking with the LORD about how much I would love to meet David Phelps. I prayed: *You know God, if I could meet David Phelps I would be very thrilled. I know You know this, but I have a little dream that one day we will get to sing together! I don't know how this is all going to get to work out but You do. If there is something in my heart that is not right or a reason I'm not supposed to meet him, then I will accept that. You are sovereign and You know everything that is best. But if I could, I would be very thrilled to meet him.*

That evening we attended the concert. David is a gifted performer and communicator. We sat down and the first half was incredible! Prior to intermission we were instructed to fill out a card and turn it in for a drawing for a free CD.

I turned to Michael rapidly and queried, "I didn't get a card when we walked in, did you?"

He said," No!"

Our plan was that during intermission we would use the bathrooms, each get a little card, fill it out and meet back in the sanctuary. So we did that. And as we sat back down I immediately turned to my husband. As the lights dimmed and the concert was about to resume, I whispered to him, "Honey, I just want you to know that I'm going to win the free drawing!"

"What do you mean?" He asked.

I continued in a hushed tone "Well, when they call the name, I don't want you to freak out because it's going to be ME! I just want you to know now!"

Michael just shrugged his shoulders a bit and had a look of whatever! He's very accustomed to me.

David Phelps came back out on stage and sang a few more songs. Then he introduced his band and backup singers. One of his backup singers, Sherry was his sister and he commented, "She has curly hair just like I do."

There was a big galvanized bin right by his feet and he looked at it and said, "Oh Sherry! Why don't you just reach down in there right now before I forget. Pull out a card for the drawing for a free CD. So she pulled one out and handed it to him.

He slowly read, "Rachel?" Then a pause. "Somebody who needs to write more clearly." I clearly wrote my name. I just don't think people know what to do with my last name, Inouye. They don't know what that is and they don't know how to pronounce Inouye.

I'm a little embarrassed to say this, but I forgot that I was 40 something at the time. I thought I was about twelve years old. So I STOOD UP like a jack-in-the-box pops up! I started shouting the spelling of my last name with my hands cupped on both sides of my mouth to be heard more clearly and increase the volume.

"I-N-O-U-Y-E !" then I sprinted toward the stage! I was so excited! This TV friend of mine, this tenor whose voice I love and who I admire, was calling me up to receive my free CD. I ran to the stage! I just lost my mind. I totally forgot what was happening. It could've been Rachel Jones or it could've been Rachel Smith but I KNEW it was ME! I did find out later, from my husband, that David continued to read our full address, house number, street and city. I am thankful for that because I just excitedly rushed the stage. I got up close to the stage but I didn't go on it. I just perched on the little steps like a little doggie with its paws up, panting, waiting for a treat from its master.

So David's sister stood in the direction facing me and she could clearly see me on the steps waiting from her vantage point. She pointed, index finger extended, she said, "David, she's right there!"

"What?" he asked?

She whispered, head tilted a bit as if to speak to him alone and not to the whole audience, and she nodded in my direction, "She's...right there!"

He didn't know what to do. What was he going to say? Go sit down?

"Come here!" he said. As he tilted his head, he made a circular motion with his hand and forearm, beckoning me toward him. Then he gave me a typical Christian side hug, the way men do. I was so excited to meet him!

He commented,"I know you!"

But I corrected, "No, no you don't. We've never met."

You see I would know if I had met him. I think he is incredibly talented and I would remember because I think he's wonderful!

On the way home, as my husband drove he repeatedly shook his head. With both hands on the steering wheel I just saw him wag his head back and forth.

"What?" I asked.

Looking at the road and not really looking at me he said, "You crack me up!"

As we drove a little further and he started laughing again.

"WHAT?" I demanded.

"I just can't believe you rushed the stage!"

The following December, my brother-in-law David handled the logistics for a David Phelps Christmas concert held in Iowa. He told me that as they set up the product table together he asked Mr. Phelps if he remembered me.

"Uh, David, I'm just wondering if you remember back in June when you were in the Milwaukee area, do you remember this gal that came...?"

He was unable to complete his question because David Phelps interrupted him saying, "I will NEVER forget it! We have changed the way that we do that whole raffle drawing."

You see, I didn't realize that all he wanted to do was say, "You are the winner of a CD and AFTER the concert you can go to the product table and pick up your free CD." I just rushed the stage and ran up to meet him there! I was so in awe.

I ask myself this question, and I guess I'm asking you too. Is this a picture of how excitedly we run into the presence of God? Are we in awe of Him? Of how He "performs" in all of creation? How He works in our lives and demonstrates Himself in nature? Are we excited to be with Him and be in His presence? Are we excited because we have talked to other people about Him? Because we have studied Him? Because we have read about Him? You see, I want that picture of how I quickly ran into the presence of a 'star' to be the way I run into the presence of my God.

One of my life verses says this: *O God, you are my God, earnestly I seek you; my soul thirsts for you, my body longs for you, in a dry and weary land where there is no water. I have seen you in the sanctuary and beheld your power and glory. Because your love is better than life, my lips will glorify you. I will praise you as long as I live, and in your name I will lift up my hands. My soul will be satisfied as with the riches of foods; with singing lips my mouth will praise you. Psalm 63:1-5*

Could this be our prayer?

Father, we stand in awe of You today. You are a holy God. You are the holy God to whom all praise is due. You are Alpha and Omega; You know the beginning from the end. You are our Protector and Provider. Our Defender-You are our shield. Our Deliverer-You fight against our enemies. And You are the Friend that Sticks closer than a Brother. I pray that the eyes of our hearts would always be open to You and who You are. I pray with David from Psalm 115: "Not to us, O LORD, not to us but to your name be glory, because of your love and faithfulness."

Let's run excitedly into His presence. He will say, "I know you!" More than a free CD, he gives us free salvation and life to the fullest.

Twenty-nine

God Doesn't Make Junk

Years ago, while I hunted for something in my jewelry drawer, I found my childhood silver-plated ID bracelet. As I held and examined it a bit, I remembered that it had seemed larger as a kid. Now, it looked so dinky. I opened the jaw-like clasp and tried it on. Wow! it still fits! I read each line stamped into its metal just like a soldier's dog tags. First my name was listed, Rachel Heggen, followed by my home address while growing up in Iowa and then the last line…Richard Heggen. Hmm, I'm known by my father. I belong to him. I think it is important, as a believer, to know whose we are. We are our heavenly Father's too, God's daughters and sons. Scripture tells us that we can become children of God. *Yet to all who received him, to those who believed in his name, he gave the right to become children of God. (John 1:12)*. We can call him "Abba," Father, Daddy.

We can better know who we are when we rightly know whose we are. If we've received Him we have the right to become His children. We belong to Him.

Because we are God's, I believe that we should gladly celebrate who we are. Really celebrate! This is an okay thing and it does not make us arrogant. This is just agreeing with God that He made a good thing. He is the one who knit us together in our mother's womb. He made us in His image. He is God and He never makes junk. So, I will ask you. Whose view do you have of yourself? Is it God's view? Whose voice are you listening to? Is it God's? Is your identity in crisis or in Christ? One verse that comes to my mind is: *For we are God's workmanship, created in Christ Jesus to do good works, which God prepared in advance for us to do. (Ephesians 2:10).*

You are God's workmanship. One version of the same verse says you are His masterpiece. Do you believe that? Not intellectually, but in your soul? Do you view yourself as God's handiwork, His masterpiece? Do you even like yourself? Are you thankful for who you are? Do you often wonder why God made you the way He did? Do you secretly wish you were someone else?

Remember, God, your creator, made you. He has never made junk. He is God! He has a purpose and plan for each of us and He specifically designed you and me for that purpose and for His glory. We must soak in the truth that we find in His word, the Bible, because all the other voices that clamor for our attention are easy to hear. (They can be the loudest.) We can easily believe the many messages that are sent our way if we don't stop and consider, very discerningly, the messenger. We must ask, Whose voice is this and from where is this message coming?

God's word says: You are God's masterpiece! I am God's masterpiece. We are God's masterpiece, His workmanship. Let that truth sink in. One visual way God taught me this truth was through the Olympics. Maybe you watch them too. I heard God speaking to me while I watched. I like to watch the summer Olympics, especially women's gymnastics. At the end of the floor exercise routine or after the dismount off the balance beam, once the gymnast has stuck her landing, what does she do? She stands confidently with her feet together and back arched. She becomes banana shaped as she throws both of her arms above her slightly-raised head and beams proudly. You know the pose, right? Ta Dah! A moment of great fulfillment, pleasure and the grand announcement. Look what I've just done! Go ahead, look! YOU are that to the world. God's grand, Ta Dah!

The fact that the God of the universe designed and made each of us and loves us as individuals, not just collectively, but each one, blows me away. God made me! That boosts my identity and the desire to celebrate what God did in designing me. He made you too, so celebrate. We each must continue to think about this truth or it becomes lost underneath a heap of lies. The lies can get dumped on us in a huge, crushing load, or even gradually one lie at a time. Either way, we can hear the lie and accept it as truth.

We must discern lies from truth and BE AWARE. We have to watch what we are watching. (We have to listen to what we are listening to. We have to mind our minds.) Otherwise, we too easily fall prey to the lies of the enemy. Be warned and reminded: Be warned that Satan is the father of lies and the accuser of the brethren. He cannot be trusted nor should he be listened to. But be reminded that we can trust the voice of our Heavenly Father, our Abba daddy, who says that we are His chosen possessions and his masterpieces.

I searched for something in my drawer that day and found my childhood ID bracelet. What a serendipity! Because it reminded me that my name and identity is tied to my father's. That profound truth comes from searching for more than jewelry in a drawer. Yes, my name was on the bracelet, but my father's name was stamped there too. I am identified by my Father and so are you. Right now I want to plant my feet firmly on that truth, throw my hands up in the air and arch my back and smile. Ta Dah!

Thirty

Angel Carrying Donuts

I was thrilled to be invited to speak at a Women's Daybreak Retreat. Prior to the event I got a little crazy. (It was as if I trusted myself more than God; I'm ashamed to type that.) I looked on my phone maps app a few times. Okay, about three times for three different evenings. I was a bit obsessed about it.

I located the church repeatedly, first in aerial view, then 3D and then written directions too. I just wanted to make sure I wouldn't have any problem getting there. One of the coordinators had emailed me and warned me not to confuse the church address with the school of the same name. I even rechecked the map a few more times regarding that.

The morning of the Day Break Conference, I left my home. *Plenty of time to arrive.* Typed the address in my phone AGAIN. My phone freaked out and continued to flip to a different address. It was kind of blinking between addresses. *Why is my phone freaking out right now?* I knew where I was going from all my previous study the nights before, so I decided to drive. At each intersection or when stopped at a red light, I'd attempt to enter the proper address again in my phone. *I think I'm headed in the general direction.* I listened intently and followed the voice commands step-by-step. Every turn and each intersection. Soon I realized I was horribly sunk. My phone application with its lovely little, automated, voice said, "Destination on your right. You have arrived!"

NO, I HADN'T!

I was in a residential neighborhood in Brookfield, not Menomonee Falls. It's possible both towns have the same street name, but clearly I was NOT at a large church. I saw only houses, only private driveways. A very quiet residential street. NO evidence of a women's retreat. NO evidence of anything. No movement or people.

I whispered a soft prayer to Jesus, and yelled a quick text to my husband. "HELP! I think I'm lost!" As I sat in the car, I reviewed old emails about this event and I found contact information for the two retreat coordinators. I called first one then the other, but no answer for either one. *That makes sense. They're probably both at the events setting up.* Yikes! The phone call rolled to voicemail, but I hung up.

I continued east and then north on roads that were somewhat familiar to me. I glanced at my phone to check the time. While a bit hesitant to enter the address again, I tried. This time I used the address straight from the last received email. *Now, Rachel, that HAS to be the right address for the church! Hold finger down. Copy.* I located where to type in desired destination straight from the copied email. *PASTE!*

Rachel you know you shouldn't try to text and drive or look at your emails and drive! So, I pulled over into a parking lot of an unfamiliar strip mall and a corner Dunkin' Donuts. I knew I shouldn't text and drive. But I'll confess, I had been texting and driving the whole way prior to stopping at the Dunkin' Donuts. Little did I know, my traveling angel would appear near my stopped car. She carried a dozen donuts in a white box, a smaller box stacked gently on top (probably holding another half dozen donuts). Before she got into her huge, black truck, I lowered my window and asked, "Excuse me, do you happen to know where the Grace Lutheran Church in Menominee Falls is located?"

She thought for a moment. "I think that it's the one recessed from the highway quite a bit."

As she began to speak directions, I thought, *Rachel, you should be writing this down.* I scrambled quickly for the first scrap of paper I could find in my car. I found an old receipt and I flipped it over to the blank side. *That'll work!* I listened a bit distractedly while trying to get my pen to work. I tried to scrawl down as much of what she said as I could.

Of course, that's when my phone rang. I glanced down, but still tried to listen to the kind woman because I wanted to HEAR the directions. One of the coordinators names flashed on my phone as it rang lying on my lap. *Oh, I'll call back*, I decided.

I slowly pulled away from my "little angel" who still held her donuts completely flat like a prized possession. I smiled, waved and said, "Thank you!" Then I chanted the directions over and over so as to remember them, *go straight, light turn left, through the roundabout and the church should be down quite a ways on your left.*

I continued the chant as my phone rang again. The name appeared on my phone. *That's one of the coordinators!* I answered, "Hello?"

A friendly gentleman's voice responded with a hello. So I said, "Oh, hello? I just want to know if Amy has already left for the retreat?"

"I don't know. Well, I'm not sure?" he said.

"Excuse me, is Amy your wife?" I asked.

"No, I don't have a wife," He replied "I just called because you have called me a few times and I wanted to know who was trying to reach me."

"Oh brother!" I explained that the earlier series of calls must have been entered incorrectly, perhaps by mistake. "You see I was looking to try to find directions to an event I am attending. I'm so sorry." I signed off with the best, "Have a great Saturday!" I could muster in a high-pitched voice.

He responded, "Hey, thanks! You too!"

I was still trying to remember the instructions as I glanced back at the barely legible writing on the receipt.

I drove closer and closer to my hopeful destination while I continued to pray that I would actually arrive. I was still chanting the names of the streets when I heard a noise. I looked around and, out of my peripheral vision, I saw my 'angel,' the directions lady, from the Dunkin' Donuts parking lot. She had pulled alongside me in the left lane. Her window was down and she began semi-shouting over the engine noise. So a I rolled mine down too. The chilly autumn air tumbled into my lap. *Burr!*

"I got to thinking," she said, "I should give you a new set of directions, perhaps an easier way!"

I was so thankful that my traveling angel had cared enough to come find me, hunt me down, and pull along side me to give me a new set of directions.

I did exactly as she instructed and was very relieved to see each landmark she had mentioned as it came into view. Just like she said, the church was on the left a bit off the highway. The moment I pulled into the church parking lot, my cell phone rang. It was Karen, one of the retreat organizers.

She said, "I got to thinking, Rachel isn't here yet, I'll check my phone to see if she is all right. I'm sorry I missed your call."

I said, "Well, I'm pulling in right now as we speak!"

I made it in plenty of time, well before the women attending the conference anyway. I think my self-reliance, address obsession and dependence on technology was put to shame that day. But I did arrive! I was ushered in by my traveling angel!

Lord, You bless my coming and going both now and forever more! Thank you!

Thirty-One

Camera, Coffee and a Crotch Rocket!

Sundays are special to me. I love to worship God with other believers. It is also a highlight because many Sundays I get ready to go to church with my lovely daughter Grace. This morning I hollered up to her, "Hey, Panny Lu (one of her nick-names) come get ready with me in my room!" Putting make-up on together and doing our hair, while talking about whatever is on our minds, had been our routine since she was a little girl.

This June morning it seemed even sweeter because summer had begun and I thought about her transferring and going away for college in the fall. I asked Grace about her day and whether we could ride together or not. She reminded me that she was going to ride her motorcycle because it was a full day. She planned to attend worship with me, grab some lunch, go to two different photo shoots. So, as we smoothed the foundation on our faces and used the blush brushes to lightly brighten our cheeks with color, we chatted about people and life. Time flew by.

Grace, though the youngest, has always been CEO of family logistics. In fact, when she was younger, I would have to curtail her desire to boss even me around. However, I didn't want to squelch the apparent ability she had to mobilize people, think through details and timelines, so I just coached her through her supervisory role gently. As is her custom, Grace in her typical way said, "Okay, mom we have about 10 more minutes and then I need to go put my camera in my backpack and we will need to head out.

I then had a flashback to when she was just a petite, young, girl, she would say,"Mom, I heard the kitchen timer, I think it was set so that you could write out the check for our piano teacher and remind us to get on our bicycles soon for our lessons." I would glance at the clock to check the time, knowing full well that she was right.

This morning reminded me of one of those days. She let me know that I would need to take a car because she would be taking her backpack loaded with her camera for the photo shoots and hop on her motorcycle. As I listened to her comforting voice she stood before me.

Grace Elizabeth, you look so beautiful. Her long, wavy, dark brown hair falling loosely on both shoulders. Her new scarf tied perfectly around her neck as she lined her eyes and applied her mascara carefully and deliberately. "Okay, five more minutes mom!" She instructed. So, I grabbed a pen, notebook, Bible, purse and poured an iced coffee into a recycled cup. *Okay, I'm set!* I backed out of the driveway but Grace remained in the garage getting set to straddle her motorcycle and back out. I motioned to her gesturing my question, *Do you want me to follow or go ahead of you?* She shook her head, raised both hands shoulder height palms lifted upward, signifying, "I don't care you choose."

So, I backed out, waited patiently in the street so I could follow her. She descended the driveway backing out slowly. I watched as she zipped her black, leather jacket, then placed her helmet on her head with her long hair draping down her back, next she tightened each motorcycle glove, and adjusted the straps of her filled backpack. I continued to observe as Grace looked over her right shoulder to do a proper head check down the street before she pulled out. I smiled as I watched my daughter make her way up the street. I followed closely behind her.

We wound through the residential street, turned out on the highway and finally merged into the oncoming traffic of the interstate. I grinned as she weaved in and out of the lanes she chose to ride in. I followed directly behind her. Every time she signaled and switched lanes, I did too. I remained directly behind her with every move she made. I never lost sight of her or allowed her to get too far ahead. Even though she rides almost daily on her motorcycle to destinations without me, today I was her escort.

I delighted in watching her as she rode with ease down the interstate. I enjoyed watching her bend down low to be more streamlined and faster. I watched as she stretched her right, followed by her left ankle from time to time. She seemed to be stretching out any part of her body that may be cramped or fatigued or perhaps warm on this summer day.

I watched as a few people in their cars gave her a double take. As they realized, *that's a young lady driving that Honda CBR 600 F4i.* I giggled as we approached the stop light because even the way she placed her feet on the ground, to steady herself was smooth and confident, ballet-like. I followed directly behind her at every junction. I was reminded of God's incredible awareness of and delight in me.

These are a few promises that He makes:

Never will I leave you, nor forsake you.

For the Lord your God is with you where ever you go.

I will bless your coming and going both now and forever more.

Yet another promise floods my mind – The Lord watches over your life.

The Lord goes before you and is your rear guard.

That one made me chuckle.

For some reason, this morning, I felt as though Grace needed an additional rear guard. So I followed her meticulously every step of the way and did not allow any cars in between us. Whether I accompany her or not, God is with her at all times. That brings me such comfort.

We turned into the parking lot, I watched as Grace slowed down as she approached each speed bump. Next she selected a lane to find a place to park, but I went down a different one. I found an open parking spot and took it. I entered the building, headed directly to the nearest bathroom and glanced at my phone with an incoming text from Grace. It read: I'm in front with Elliot and Grace. My sweet daughter had again handled the logistics, had gone before me, selected the seats and now we could worship the King together.

Epilogue

God is always speaking. He didn't just write the Bible and become mute. He speaks to us everywhere and in ordinary, every day situations. I'll never forget the lessons he taught me through some lily pads. He said, "Rachel, do you see those lily pads?"

I looked over at them, "Yes," I answered.

"See how they lay across the water that upholds and sustains them? That's the way I am up holding you and sustaining you. Do you see how the lily pad's each touch each other? I want you to touch the lives of other people and have other people touch your life too. See the bright white water lily?"

That's when I interrupted. I said, "God, may I be the bright blooming flower?"

We had a really good conversation that day and I was taught a great deal about the spiritual through the natural. So now let me ask you, "Do you see God in everyday situations and in the ordinary things in your life?"

He is always speaking. I challenge you to look for Him and listen to Him. Recognize His voice through the everyday noise. It is an awesome treasure hunt. It maybe just a word that He wants you to grab on to. It could be that something you've recently read has an application in the natural around you. But know this, He plays seek and find not hide and seek.

Happy listening, seeking and finding! God is on display!

About The Author

Speaker, author and blogger.

Rachel's transparency and authenticity in her relationship with Christ makes an impact on the lives around her. She is a gifted communicator with great ability to articulate and apply God's Word in everyday language for everyday situations through stories and Scripture. She desires to encourage people in their relationship with God. As a former educator and home school mom, she loves teaching.

Rachel lives in Wisconsin and is married to Michael. They have two sons, Michael and Andrew, one daughter, Grace and one daughter-in-law, Amy (married to Michael). Rachel serves at Elmbrook Church, Brookfield in ministries that allow her to use her gifts. She is energetic, eager and in love with her Lord. She brings radiant enthusiasm to the things in which she is involved.

Rachel can be reached at:

rachelinouye.org
rachelinouye.wordpress.com
@4thgirlrach on Twitter
@rachelinouyespeaker on Facebook

Cover - Painting by Rachel Inouye

Back Cover Photo and Cover Layout- Michael Inouye

Photo Credits:

pg 112. Michael Inouye
pg 161. Second Mirror Photography.

Andrew Inouye.
  Second-Mirror.com
  InouyeMusic.com